NEW ZEALAND FOR TOURISTS

The Traveler's Guide to Make The Most Out of Your Trip to New Zealand - Where to Go, Eat, Sleep & Party

By Dagny Taggart

Disclaimer

The information provided in this book is designed to provide helpful information on the subjects discussed. The author's books are only meant to provide the reader with the basics travel guidelines of a certain location, without any warranties regarding the accuracy of the information and advice provided. Each traveler should do their own research before departing.

Table of Contents

Dedicated to those who love going beyond their own frontiers.

Keep on traveling,

Dagny Taggart

My FREE Gift to You!

As a way of saying thank you for downloading my book, I'd like to send you an exclusive gift that will revolutionize the way you learn new languages. It's an extremely comprehensive PDF with 15 language hacking rules that **will help you learn 300% <u>faster</u>, with <u>less effort</u>, and with <u>higher than ever retention rates</u>**.

This guide is an amazing complement to the book you just got, and could easily be a stand-alone product, but for now I've decided to give it away for free, to thank you for being such an awesome reader, and to make sure I give you all the value that I can to help you succeed faster on your language learning journey.

To get your FREE gift, go to the link below, follow the steps, and I'll send it to your email address right away.

>> <u>http://bitly.com/Language-Gift</u> <<

GET **INSTANT** ACCESS

Learn Any Language 300% FASTER

>> Get Full Online Language Courses With Audio Lessons <<

Would you like to learn a new language before you start your trip? I think that's a great idea. Now, why don't you do it 300% *FASTER*?

I've partnered with the most revolutionary language teachers to bring you the very language online courses I've ever seen. It's a mind-blowing program specifically created for language hackers such as ourselves. It will allow you learn ANY language, from French to Chinese, 3x faster, straight from the comfort of your own home, office, or wherever you may be. It's like having an unfair advantage!

You can choose from a wide variety of languages, such as French, Spanish, Italian, German, Chinese, Portuguese, and A TON more.

Each Online Course consists of:

+ 91 Built-In Lessons
+ 33 Interactive Audio Lessons
+ 24/7 Support to Keep You Going

The program is extremely engaging, fun, and easy-going. You won't even notice you are learning a complex foreign language from scratch. And before you realize it, by the time you go through all the lessons you will officially become a truly solid speaker.

Old classrooms are a thing of the past. It's time for a revolution.

If you'd like to go the extra mile, then follow the link below, and let the revolution begin!

>> http://www.bitly.com/foreign-language-courses <<

Introduction
Why You Will Fall In Love With New Zealand

New Zealand revels in its role as nature's amphitheater, the country redefining notions of the sublime and the surreal. Every turn seems to unveil a new panorama, a new aesthetic seemingly lost in time. New Zealand is unspoiled and untamed. Its status as home of fictionalized Middle Earth is well publicized, but there's far more to the landscape than hobbit holes and orcas hiding in trees. There is bounty to be discovered everywhere and almost every visitor is won over with fresh impressions of natural splendor. With more sheep than people and more solitude than city, New Zealand is a place for getting lost in the midst of the planet's most spectacular landscapes.

New Zealand essentially consists of a series of islands in the Pacific, each distinct and celebrating its difference. Two large islands dominate this definition. The volcanic North Island, full of rolling green pastures and kaleidoscopic color. And the mountainous South Island, home to glaciers, fjords, and dramatic geological features. While the land provides an omnipresent highlight, there's more to New Zealand than a journey through lakes, mountains, ocean, and forests dancing with phantasmal intrigue.

The country runs on an indelibly laid-back rhythm, one that negates the use of a watch and helps you easily slip into the natural spell. You could travel a hundred miles without seeing another person and most settlements still retain the unpopulated charm of yesteryear. Such rurality inevitably supports a famed local friendliness. Everyone has time to say hello and greet a stranger and rushing around is a serious no no. Stress, it seems, disappears the moment you land in the country. Even a journey that traverses the whole of New Zealand will be defined by serenity.

This guidebook has a very New Zealand approach at heart. It likes to keep things simple and tranquil, preferring not to dampen the journey with layer after layer of purposeless information. This is a country that must be discovered. We would prefer to leave enough for you to discover when you arrive. At the same time, the helping hand of a local guide is essential for navigating the best the country has to offer. So think of this guidebook as the friendly locals you meet in New Zealand, full of tips and ideas but always leaving the final decision to you. In this guidebook we detail all the iconic and unmissable experience, as well as all the hidden and off the beaten track ideas that should be considered.

This complete planning guide presents destinations from a visitor's perspective. Rather than use local administrative regions, the guidebook is split into key routes and regions that are easy to explore from a single base. Using this approach enables a clear overview of what's possible when you visit New Zealand, and which destinations are effortlessly combined in an itinerary.

What this guidebook doesn't do, is fill two pages with hotels and restaurants with less than complimentary descriptions. If it's good and worth experiencing then it's in this guidebook. If it's not then it didn't make the cut. There's more than enough enchantment and quality to find in New Zealand, why dilute it with the mundane? So jump forward and jump in to a country that captures the imagination and stirs the intrepidness in every soul. Welcome to New Zealand and welcome to a country that always leaves a lasting impression.

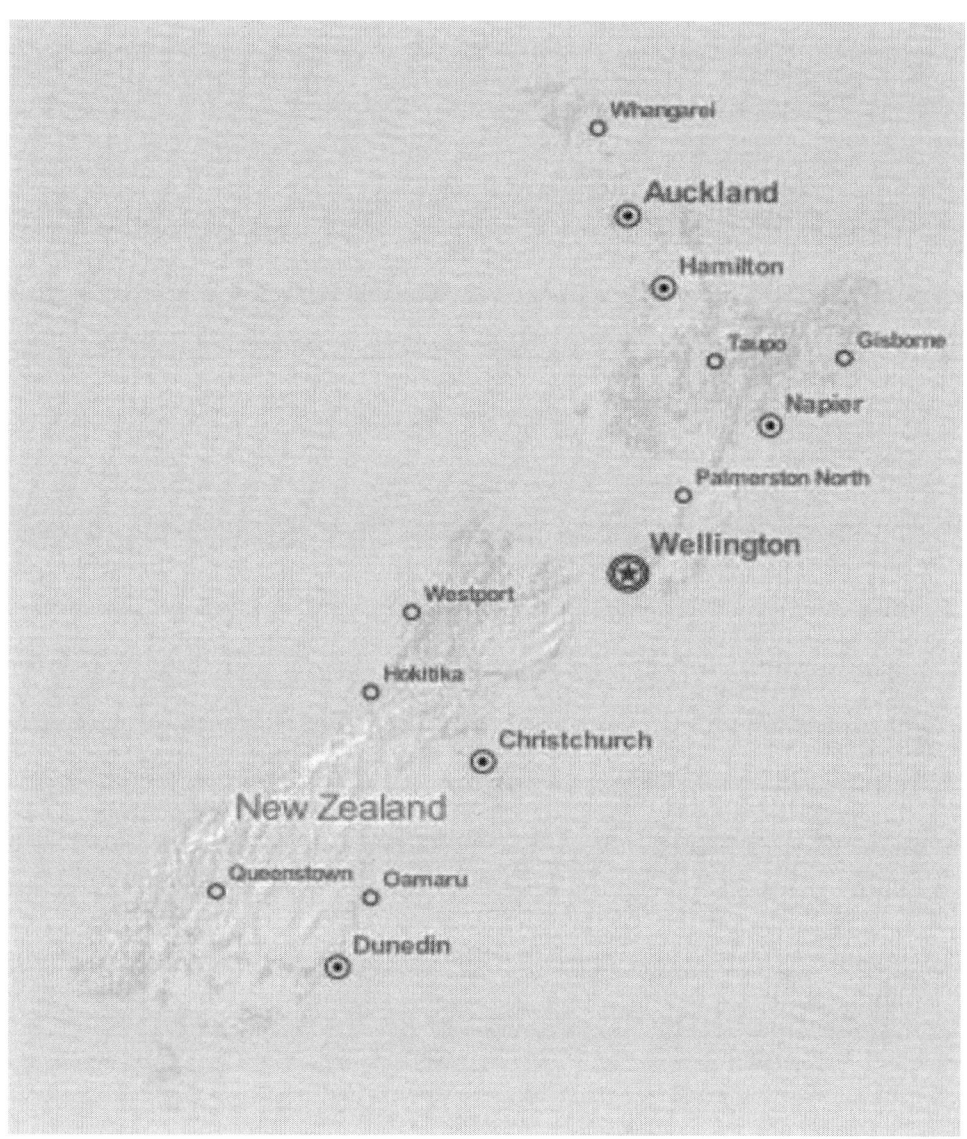

©Openstreetmap Contributors

11

Chapter 1
Welcome to New Zealand!

New Zealand at a glance

A few hidden islands aside, New Zealand can be thought about as a North and South Island. Cast adrift in the South Pacific, both these islands imbue impressions of trademark natural beauty and tranquility. They're similarly sized, small enough to cross in a single day (albeit a long one) yet big enough to spend two months exploring and not get close to experiencing it all. Both are equally attractive for slightly different reasons. Some visitors prefer to concentrate on one or the other, exploring in more depth and fully soaking up the experience on offer. Other visitors will find additional beauty in the contrast, choosing instead to pick a handful of destinations across both islands.

The North Island has a volcanic history and the lava still spills out of its active domes. It's a green and peculiar landscape, marked by rolls and curves and pastures. Nothing is flat until you reach the coast and dozens of miles of beach roll into the Pacific. The South Island geology is more dramatic; mountains rise in rugged triangles, fjords and glaciers are dappled by white, and there's even less flat space. Naturally, it's colder here and less green. But that's compensated by panoramas that are difficult to rival anywhere else on the planet.

While the atmosphere is one of quaint backwater, this is a developed Western nation with a sophisticated tourist infrastructure. Moving between islands and destinations is easy and straightforward. Roads are in excellent condition (and almost completely devoid of traffic), airlines connect major destinations and towns, and hundreds of tour companies can provide a safe adventure into ethereal landscapes. Hotels harmoniously blend with their surroundings and always provide space (no cramped hovels here) and medical facilities are amongst the best in the world. In short, there's no limit to the adventure on offer, other than your own spirit. Here are a few experiences to get you excited...

Iconic Experiences

- Most journeys will have your eyes lost in a mystical haze and this feeling of incredulity is epitomized by **Milford Sound**, a narrow fjord surrounded by dramatic mountains that empties into the Tasman Sea. It's part of the **Fjordland National Park**, which in turn is one of seven national parks that cover the **West Coast of the South Island**.

- New Zealand is **Middle Earth** and parts of the whole country formed part of Peter Jackson's Lord of the Rings trilogy. The movie themed reverie is showcased at **Hobbiton** and hundreds of other sites across the country. However, it's also easy to discover your own Middle Earth, especially with one of the country's three **cross island rail journeys.**

- Indigenous **Maoris** staunchly defended their land and helped preserve the country from colonial pillagers. Their culture is best found on the North Island and **Rotorua**, a place of exploding geysers, authentic war dances, and effervescent traditions.

- All across New Zealand you'll find **lakes**, each of them fringed by bucolic landscapes and providing the base for both relaxing and adventure. Losing a few days on the lakeshore is part of the local experience, as is kayaking or jet boating across one.

- **Mountains** inevitably play a strong role in most New Zealand experiences. The South Island has a **winter ski season** as well as some of the planet's most evocative multi-day mountain **hiking trails (**in particular the **Milford and Healy tracks)**. On the North Island you'll find dozens of destinations for a day in the hills or on top of a peak. In fact, with literally dozens of national parks and forest reserves, it's difficult to go a day without finding a new set of hiking and **mountain bike trails**.

- **Queenstown** loves its self-made reputation as adrenalin capital of the world. This is where the world's first commercial bungee jump was swung up and it's added to by swings, zip lining, parasailing, and just about anything else to get the heart racing. The mood is infectious, and it's also fun just to watch the ecstatic faces.

Queenstown provides both adrenalin and serenity.

Unique Experiences

- Travel to the very north of the North Island and your eyes begin to cry in happiness at the sight of **Ninety Mile Beach**. Yes, it's pretty much this long, and a wonderful journey that seems to take you to the edge of the world.

- Glaciers are normally reserved for serious climbers but irrevocable shapes of ice are open to the lay tourist on the west of the South Island. **Franz Josef Glacier and Fox Glacier** flow through rainforest and tumble into the ocean, and they offer very unique opportunities to explore.

- **Traveling by helicopter** is normally an indulgence too costly to even consider. New Zealand isn't any cheaper than elsewhere in the world, but the aerial visual rewards mean that it's an experience than even the poorest traveler will consider.

- Take a boat to **White Island**, an active volcano that's still bubbling with primitive majesty. Put on a gas mask and you can trek to the very edge of the crater, where the hissing and bubbling always leaves goosebumps.

- New Zealand **wine** is slowly emerging on the international scale, spearheaded by the **Marlborough** and **Central Otago** regions. A sensual journey through the vineries provides another excuse to indulge in the landscapes.

14

How To Use This Guide

This guide is split into three distinct sections, each building on the last and ensuring you're fully prepped for a trip to New Zealand. As previously mentioned, this isn't a guidebook that's choked by endless listings of restaurants, bars, and hotels. New Zealand is an easy country to travel in. The locals speak English, tourist establishments are everywhere, and you're often left in one of two situations: there's only one choice, or there's so much choice your mind bristles with delight. This guidebook sticks to the essential information, providing what you need to effectively plan and travel to New Zealand. It's not going to hold your hand and recommend ordering the lamb chops because the burger sometimes comes with too much sauce. It is going to fully prepare you for the country and ensure you can maximize your time and enjoyment here.

By providing a broad overview of everything on offer, this guidebook is designed with the every visitor in mind. Idiosyncratic attractions are included as are the experiences that make New Zealand absolutely unique. But it doesn't linger on the details of 40 different hiking trails. Likewise, rather than list all the different hotels and guesthouses, the guidebook prefers to direct you to the best up to date sources of information.

Chapter 2 is all about planning your trip. It discusses potential routes and itineraries, when to go, how much money you're going to need, how to get there, and the basic travel requirements. You'll find a whole section on getting around and planning your transport, as well as a section on getting the best value and managing your costs. Chapter 2 is also where to come for information about where you're going to sleep and the different accommodation to find in New Zealand.

Chapter 3 is about maximizing your experience in the country and ensuring you don't miss out. What's the local food like, what will you order in a bar, which manners are essentially to know, and how do you ensure you're always safe? This chapter is about immersing yourself in New Zealand and squeezing every last piece of charm from the country.

The rest of the chapters provide detailed information about destinations in New Zealand. They're divided geographically, starting with the north of the North Island and continuing to the...well, it's kind of obvious where you're going to end up by the end of the guidebook. New Zealand doesn't have many roads. Visitors are generally restricted to a series of routes along the country's state highways. Each destination chapter lists destinations geographically along these routes, enabling a clear picture of which destinations can be combined.

With each destination you're introduced to the place and the experiences on offer, enabling you to make a succinct and informed decision about whether it's somewhere for your itinerary. Then the guide goes into more detailed practical information that turn a dreamy visit into firm reality; if you need to know about it, it will be covered in our *travel essentials*.

Chapter 2
Planning Your Trip Ahead(Travel Routes, Itineraries, Etc)

The biggest consideration when planning a New Zealand trip is whether to explore one or both islands. Both offer a distinct experience although both imbue the same impressions of New Zealand's laid-back atmosphere. This chapter is split into North and South Island ideas to give a picture of what is on offer.

Classic Routes at a Glance

One Week North: A week is long enough to cross the North Island from Auckland to Wellington or vise versa. There's three main available, the most popular being traversing through the center of the island. A week is long enough to also take in a day trip to the attractions north of Auckland.

One Week South: Either land in Queenstown and spend a week in the south of the island, exploring the West Coast national parks and a rugged land-scape of mountains and lakes. From here there's a loop back to Queenstown via Christchurch. Another option is to travel from Queenstown up to Christ-church, passing through Mt Cook National Park.

An example of a state highway in New Zealand.

One Week North and South: Fly between destinations and get a flavor of the diversity by exploring Queenstown, Rotorua, and then your choice of city.

Two Weeks North: With two weeks you can really explore. Head north from Auckland to the Bay of Islands and Ninety Mile Beach, cross the volcanic center and its national parks, and check out hidden beaches on one of the coastlines. There's also the opportunity to complete a loop from Auckland to Wellington and back.

Two Weeks South: There's enough time to experience most of the island, from the fjords and national parks around Queenstown all the way up to Abel Tasman National Park and the vineyards of Marlborough. However, you'll still need to be selective and perhaps use flights to minimize travel time.

Two Weeks North and South: Divide your time equally and look at the classic routes above for one week on each island.

Three Weeks North and South: Three weeks ensures a true impression of the country's diversity. The above routes should provide ideas and then there's the off the beaten track places to discover, like outlying islands, remote national parks, and lazing away a few days on a beach or lakeside.

Creating Your Itinerary

Every visitor to New Zealand is likely to forge their own itinerary. This isn't a country for following a set must-see list of destinations and attractions. The second greatest consideration when traveling here is how to find more time. Almost everyone leaves New Zealand wishing they had more time to spend, and that's true regardless if you have a week or three months. This isn't a country for rushing around and trying to tick off as much as possible. If time is short then it's far easier to absorb the country's beauty by limiting the destinations.

It wouldn't fit the New Zealand style to thickly detail an exact itinerary. In a country of discovery, there are dozens of different places to stop. However, the limited number of roads means there's only a few possible routes, especially when heading through the mountains. The destination sections are presented along the lines of these major routes. There are some overarching considerations when planning any itinerary.

- **Winding roads and travel time:** Picture an ultra straight American desert highway. Now picture its opposite. That's a New Zealand road, winding, rolling, turning, meandering, and never allowing the speedometer to wobble very high. So a 120 mile journey between destinations will probably take at least three hours, and that's not including the numerous photo stops on route. If you're going by road, try not to over-estimate how fast you can travel.

- **Domestic flights:** A well-established network of local flights now connect much of the country, effortlessly minimizing travel time and always providing great views from the window. They're also cheap. Just utilizing a couple of these can really expand your options.

- **New Zealand's diversity:** Many people arrive in New Zealand and, thanks to a mix of clever marketing and global preconceptions, think that they've found Middle Earth. But they could all be looking at a different view. The country offers a mix of mountain, forest, beach, city, volcano, green hills,

19

lakes, glacier, and a dozen other ecosystems. You can't see it all. But consider combining a range of these backdrops regardless of how short your visit is.

- **Think about the weather:** It's a long way from north to south and the climatical variations are huge. Thinking about the weather when you visit should form a strong part of your itinerary planning.

When To Go and Understanding Different Seasons

New Zealand's weather has a terrible reputation, especially if you ask anyone from Australia. While this isn't a country for endless days sunbathing, myths about continual rain are far off the mark. The country's weather reputation usually stems from a few isolated destinations. These are remote Pacific Islands after all, so you should expect a few crazy anomalies. For example, there are parts of the South Island's West Coast that receive a whopping ten meters of rainfall a year. But head 200 miles east and the annual precipitation is more like one meter a year.

The natural geography forges a remarkable climatical diversity and there's often the need to pack for all eventualities. This diversity means there is no bad time to go. It's not like you'll miss the main attraction if you can only travel in summer. Regardless of the month, there will be somewhere in prime visiting season. Despite this talk of weather superlatives, New Zealand officially has a mellow climate, rarely reaching searing temperatures or plunging to sub-zero lows. Here's a rough guide to the weather and what's happening when you want to go.

Summer (December to February)
Warmest and clearest weather across most of the country but this peak season sees prices rise and quiet retreats get busy.
This is easily the hottest time of year and unquestionably peak season for tourism in New Zealand. In particular, mid-December to the end of January is the local school holiday period so expect an increase in prices and remote idyllic retreats to be buzzing with families. Arrive in summer and the beaches also become great to visit, temperatures are consistently between 65 and 85°F and there's nowhere that isn't accessible.

Fall (March to May)
Great time to visit all of New Zealand, just remember to pack for all seasons.

Fall brings just about every type of weather to the country. Expect sun, wind, rain, cloud, and everything in between. As the country heads out of summer the landscapes are imbued with shimmering new shades of color – a further dimension to your Middle Earth portrait. It's a good time of year to visit both islands but bring a good jumper.

Winter (June to August)

Snow in the south and wet in the north. Off peak season so cheaper prices and few other people around.

Queenstown's ski slopes provide another reason to visit New Zealand and you'll find the snow during the winter months. The skies are usually clear and crisp on the South Island but the temperature goes sub-zero and parts of the island become inaccessible. The North Island isn't as cold although the weather isn't always that pleasant. Still, bring a good coat and the country is virtually yours, outside the ski slopes. Winter is low season in New Zealand and this is also the cheapest time to travel.

Spring (September to November)

The wettest season but also the most diverse and a chance to combine every-thing on offer.

The regular rain in spring is offset by the blossoming landscapes. All countries look better in the spring bloom, and that's magnified in New Zealand. While rain can be off putting, this is the best season to completely explore the country's diversity. While the last days of snow are enjoyed in the South, the beaches of the North start to welcome back sunbathers (albeit brave ones).

The tiny village of Paradise, South Island, in August.

Travel Costs and Organizing Your Money

New Zealand isn't a budget country. For starters, wherever you call home is thousands of miles from this forgotten corner of the world map. So flights are going to be pricey. With so many tours and activities to cover it's unsurprising that New Zealand becomes a destination to really save for and experience once in a lifetime. Having said that, New Zealand doesn't need to be overly expensive. It's easy to eat and travel relatively cheaply if you're prepared to cook your own meals and stick to what is excellent quality budget accommodation. Here is a brief overview.

Example Budgets for a New Zealand Trip

The information here is a very rough guide and designed to be used purely for planning purposes. Further consideration must be placed on how much time you have. If you're cramming a lot into a week or two then plan on at least an additional 25% to the figures below. If you're taking it slow and moving about less then subtract 25%.

- **Budget traveler (US$ 70 - 90 a day)** – You can achieve this by sleeping in hostels, cooking most of your meals, being selective over tours, and not hammering the bars. The hardest part of staying within budget is turning down some of the tours and activities on offer. You can live off $40 a day. But a Milford Sound day tour will then cost over $100. So check for the free activities in national parks, like the innumerable hiking trails.

- **Conscientious traveler ($90 - 120 a day)** – Extra money in the budget is usually spent on doing a few more tours and activities, as well as eating out more often. With the quality of budget accommodation being so high, it's not necessarily worth splashing the cash on more expensive hotels.

- **Standard traveler ($120 - 150 a day)** – With a budget in this range you can afford to really enjoy yourself. It should allow a good mid-range hotel, eating out one or two times a day, having a few drinks, and going on most of the tours.

- **Upmarket traveler ($150 - 250)** – Start spending more and New Zealand is unveiled in increasingly boutique style. There should be nothing on your bucketlist that can't be achieved and the higher range hotels add extra charm to the trip.

- **Luxury traveler ($250+)** - Traveling in style can mean the country's most expensive hotels. In New Zealand it also means the country's most unique experiences. Think helicopter rides, private islands, white water rafting down secluded rivers, and all the other things that come from the annals of adventure travel reverie.

Example Costs in New Zealand

- Here's an idea of what day to day New Zealand is going to cost you (all prices in US$).

- Dorm bed / private double room in a good hostel - $20 / 60

- Double room in a mid-range hotel - $60 – 100

- Meal for two at a good but not gourmet restaurant - $50 – 80

- Journey of 200 miles by public transport - $20 – 30

- Full day tour of famous natural attraction – anywhere from $70 – 150

- Pint of beer in a local bar - $7 – 10

- Takeaway sandwich lunch from a cafe - $10 - 15

Easy Ways to Reduce Your Costs When Traveling in New Zealand

New Zealand is often a once in a lifetime vacation so everybody will want enough money to do it properly. Traveling all the way to the south of the South Island and then being unable to afford a trip to the West Coast National Parks really sucks. So here are a few easy tips for cutting the costs and ensuring you don't miss out.

- **Be selective and plan your tours:** At just about every destination there's going to be a list of awesome sounding tours dangling before your eyes. Do them all and the credit card will be maxed before you've left Auckland.

Try doing some pre-planning and be selective, ensuring you've got the money leftover for tours later in your trip.

- **Enjoy the free stuff:** New Zealand is about outdoor adventures and in many places this shouldn't cost you anything. National parks are usually free to enter and you've got thousands of miles of hiking trails and the like to enjoy.

- **Avoid peak season:** Mid-December to end-January is just about the only time when hotels will be full and the destinations will really cash in with inflated prices. Avoid these times and you could save 50%, including with your international airfare.

- **Take advantage of online offers:** New Zealand may have a backwater ambiance but it's on the web and there's some great cut price deals to be found online.

- **Cook your own meals:** Everyone raves about local produce and going eco these days. New Zealand is exactly that, a country eating its own meat and locally grown vegetables. There's excellent quality food to be found in the shops and cooking it yourself is going to be cheaper and better than heading out for another budget fast food fry up.

- **Rent a car:** With so much of New Zealand lying off the beaten track this is a country that really rewards self-drive trips. It takes you to new places and opens up destinations with great budget hotels.

- **Book buses in advance:** New Zealand's long distance buses have a confusing pricing system that rewards fastidious planners. Pay for your ticket 90 days in advance and you cross an island for $1. The same journey might be $60 when a ticket is purchased on the day.

Organizing Your Money

The New Zealand dollar is usually a little weaker than its neighboring Australian dollar, and generally worth around 0.75 – 0.85 of the US dollar. It's not always plain sailing when trying to spend your money though. Visa and Mastercard are beginning to catch on, but this is by no means universal. Upmarket tourist establishments will certainly take them. However, you'll need cash to buy lunch at a Mom and Pop cafe along the road. ATM's will accept almost any foreign card, but you may be traveling 150 miles between them. So when heading into rural area, try and stock up on the dollars. Currency exchange can be found in any place likely to receive a good stream of tourists, with Australian and American dollars the easiest to change.

Basic Travel Requirements

EU, American, and Canadian citizens are on the New Zealand visa waiver list. That means there's no visa required if you're coming for a vacation and staying less than three months (six months for UK citizens). Those from other countries should check the New Zealand immigration website - www.*immigration*.govt.*nz*/

Immigration officials can be very strict about checking that you've come on vacation. With a large young immigrant workforce from around the world, they're not to keen on people turning up without a plan. To be classed as a tourist you'll need to have an onward or return flight. If you don't have one, there's a good chance you won't be allowed to board a plane to New Zealand. Once you arrive, having a print off of your ticket and travel itinerary often smoothes over any over-zealous questioning.

New Zealand has been trying to restrict foreign flora and fauna for hundreds of years. Many of its native species have become endangered as imported wildlife has arrived and gobbled up all the resources (the kiwi has almost disappeared). When you arrive, you'll be asked to declare any foreign material. That doesn't mean porn or marijuana. It means things like a banana in your bag, some left over raisins, or yesterday's lunch hiding in a backpack. Use the honesty bins to dump anything that might be contraband on arrival. There's strict and hefty fines for not doing so. And a squashed banana really isn't worth $500.

Getting to New Zealand

New Zealand is rather inconveniently situated, tucked away in the corner of the world map and seemingly a million miles from anywhere. Even a flight from Australia is going to take at least three hours. Auckland is the largest and busiest of the airports and it's situated in the north of the North Island. Christchurch (South Island) and Wellington (North Island) are also popular international airports. The fourth option is Queenstown, the tourist hub in the south of the South Island. There are less flights here but it's most convenient for the Fjordlands and ski season.

The relatively low cost of local flights invariably means that the most cost effective way to reach New Zealand is to find the cheapest ticket to anywhere in the country. Christchurch offers direct routes across the Pacific to South America while Auckland is served by over 20 airlines. New Zealand is a country of islands and there aren't any commercial options for going by water or overland.

Getting Around New Zealand

Getting around New Zealand is never tiresome. Every journey is part of the experience, whether it's flying above fjords, taking a train to Middle Earth, or rolling along curved mountain roads. It's the journeys that showcase untrammeled New Zealand at its finest, so think of this section less of getting around, and more of an essential part of your New Zealand experience. In a laid-back country it pays to be flexible and utilizing a range of transport options is likely to offer the best value for money when getting around the country.

Suburban City Transport

Most New Zealand cities and towns are barely big enough to warrant a bus service and you won't need to decipher any confusing underground metro maps. Suburban bus services are generally reliable but infrequent and the proximity of everything means that taxis and two legs are often the best ways to go. Auckland and Wellington have commuter trains although it's rare that visitors use them.

Scheduled Long Distance Bus Services

Long distance coach travel is an easy way to get around the country and a range of competing bus companies provide intercity services. It's very comfortable and can be very cheap if you book in advance. Ticket prices can start at just $1 if you're booking 90 days in advance. However, get a ticket on the day and expect to pay significantly more. The buses are cheaper than trains and connect almost all of New Zealand's destinations, including those remote places with a population of 100 plus farm animals. Major companies include Intercity (www.intercity.co.nz), Naked Bus (nakedbus.com) and Mana Bus, for the North Island only (www.manabus.com).

Buses are reliable and you can expect dazzling vistas through the window. The downside is their frequency. Even services between major destinations may only depart once a day, which can be restrictive and lead to unsociable departure or arrival times.

Hop On Hop Off Tourist Bus Services

The mainstay of New Zealand's youth travel industry has been hop on hop off bus services. The distinction between bus service and guided tour is increasingly blurred and decoding the various products and routes on offer can be a challenge. The Kiwi Experience were the first (www.kiwiexperience.com), and they've been joined by Stray Travel Bus (www.straytravel.com) and Magic Bus (www.magicbus.co.nz). In addition, Intercity, the country's largest bus operator, offers flexible and fixed itinerary bus passes, an excellent option if you're in the country for one week or more.

The challenge with choosing a bus company is you can't try before you buy. It makes financial sense to choose a travel pass with one company. So what's the difference and how do you make sense of it all? If you're looking for the greatest flexibility and plan to make more than a three or four bus journeys than the Intercity passes make sense. There are more routes, more services, and more choice. The Kiwi Experience and its recent competitors appeal to more of a backpacker audience. It's only tourists on board and you'll stop at viewpoints on route as the trip merges bus service with guided journey. Having said that, it can be more expensive and slower. During the off season, the competition to get bums on seats means you can pick up some excellent bargains if you're flexible.

Hiring a Vehicle

Driving is easy in New Zealand. There's hardly anything on the road (other than stray sheep) and the roads are in excellent condition. Even the most remote mountain passes are unlikely to require four wheel drive, so the ultra budget hire car can get you around. For flexibility and experiencing off the beaten track New Zealand this is a popular and cost effective choice. Healthy competition has kept prices reasonable and fuel isn't going to wipe out your credit card.

There are more options than renting a car. Motorhome rental is increasingly popular and the plethora of public campsites make this an attractive option for anyone with a month or more in New Zealand. Perhaps the cheapest of all options is to hire a car and to sleep at these public campsites. Motorbike rental is also popular with the insatiable combination of empty roads through glorious landscapes and modern bikes.

Empty roads are the main feature of almost every New Zealand journey.

The major disadvantage to hiring a vehicle is the Cook Straight, the narrow strip of water separating the North and South Islands. Taking a vehicle on the boat is expensive, as is the one way rental price for dropping a vehicle off on the other island. It usually works out cheaper to rent a vehicle in the North, then rent a different vehicle in the South. Achievable loops can be made around each island from any of the four major international airports (Auckland, Wellington, Christchurch, and Queenstown). Then fly to the other island and pick up a new vehicle at the airport.

Internal Flights

Domestic flights form part of most New Zealand itineraries. Book a few weeks in advance and there's a good chance that it's cheaper to fly than to take the bus. In particular, airlines provide the easiest and quickest way to navigate the Cook Straight and travel between the islands. Jetstar offer the budget airline option (www.jetstar.com) while Air New Zealand has the most extensive network (www.airnewzealand.co.nz). Sounds Air (www.soundsair.com) and Air2there (www.air2there.com) offer limited routes around Wellington and the south of the North Island.

Domestic flights seem to epitomize the New Zealand ambiance. There are no queues to go through security (and no daft rules about not bringing liquids on board), turning up with just 30 minutes to spare is the norm, and you often walk onto the tarmac at a near deserted airport.

Train Travel

Visitors are usually torn on their opinion of New Zealand's rail services. Privatization essentially closed most of the country's rural rail network and the rail operators firmly focus their services on tourists. If you like train travel then you're in for a treat. The three remaining routes slowly wind into dramatic landscapes, dissecting rural New Zealand and offering glorious vistas through the large windows. You can essentially travel from Auckland all the way down and across to Greymouth (or vise versa) using the three train lines:

- Greymouth to Christchurch on the TranzAlpine – this is a four hour mountain journey west to east on the South Island.

- Christchurch to Picton on the Coastal Pacific service timed to meet the ferry across the Cook Straight – this runs up the East Coast of the South Island.

- Wellington to Auckland on the Northern Explorer – traversing almost the full length of the North Island.

These are some of the world's most scenic train journeys. But they're expensive and slow. If sitting on a train and watching the world go by isn't your cup of tea, then you're probably better taking the bus and arriving in half the time. There's no need to scour the timetables for the best departure times. The Northern Explorer runs on alternate days and the other services only run once a day.

Riding a Bike

There has been an advantage to the closure of rail services. As of early 2015, a single bike route connects the far north to the far south of New Zealand, the majority of the trail built on the disused rail track. For the adventurous it's an idyllic opportunity to experience the country's rugged hinterlands.

Crossing the Cook Straight

Travel to both main islands and you'll need to cross the Cook Straight, an often stormy body of water fringed by a canopy of green forest. There are 9 – 10 daily sailings between Wellington and Picton, operated by Interislander (www.interislander.co.nz) and Bluebridge (www.bluebridge.co.nz). They operate large comfortable boats and the journey takes 3.5 hours. Booking a ticket isn't always straightforward given the choice of superfare, flexifare, confusingfare, and makesureyoubookinadvancefare. In short, book in advance and it's around NZ$55 for a journey but you're stuck to a single ferry. Turn up on the day and it's more like NZ$80.

Given the time it takes and the price, many people choose to fly between the islands instead.

Where to Stay

The country of the Hobbit Hole always has distinctive accommodation.

New Zealand's accommodation seems to have formed a blueprint the rest of the world's unknowingly followed. "Boutique" and "eco" are major buzzwords in the tourism industry, with the use of one of the other practically guaranteeing double the customers paying double the price. New Zealand has been boutique and eco for long before the terms garnered fashionability. Converted farmhouses, Mom and Pop guesthouses in tiny villages, hand-crafted hotels in cities...New Zealand's accommodation is as distinctive as the landscape it graces. Unsurprising given that this is the home of Hobbit Holes. Always expect space. In a country of just a few million people, cramming things together never made any sense. Budget hotel rooms are far bigger than what you would find elsewhere in the world and 4* hotels are likely to feel more like private villas.

The New Zealand style is to be low key and intimate. Gleaming luxury hotels wouldn't sit comfortably in such unspoiled surroundings and there's little use of flashing Chinese neon or polished exteriors. While the major hotel chains are represented, you're likely to find better value and a more local feel in the vast numbers of owner managed guesthouses and hotels. Small boutique hotels play a major role in most itineraries and there's always something cute and endearing to remember. Breakfasts are invariably included and are often hearty affairs, blending the colonial English style of frying everything with healthier local options – fresh yoghurt, smoked salmon, etc.

Individual destinations always provide their own touches, from sheep wandering around outside to views over Auckland Harbour from the sixth floor (a height that imbues skyscraper status in New Zealand). Views over inspiring landscapes are omnipresent outside the cities and locations can provide full immersion in the escapist rurality.

Booking in advance is essential in cities with hotels often having a walk in rate that's far above what you can find online. All the major hotel booking sites can help you get a good deal (e.g. www.booking.com and www.tripadvisor.com). Outside the cities and major towns, small guesthouses and bed and breakfasts make a living on passing trade. For example, arrive in a village after dusk and all might be quiet at the guesthouse. Knock on the door, keep knocking, then an old woman opens up with a feverish smile and you get a cup of tea before seeing a spacious double room with views onto the mountain. Especially with your own vehicle, not planning and booking in advance adds some extra charm to the adventure.

Star ratings are not as meticulously followed as elsewhere in the world. If a place doesn't have one, that's no indication that is doesn't deserve one. Here's an overview of the options and prices when traveling in New Zealand. Prices are in US$.

Hostels ($20 – 30pp) – New Zealand's hostels are better quality than the standard preconception of bedbugs and couples getting on in the dorm above your head. Facilities and amenities are good and there's far more space than squeezing into an apartment in some European capital. Some also offer wonderfully scenic locations on hidden beaches or in thick forests. While the quality is good enough for almost everyone, the crowd is generally young and party focused, particularly in major destinations. All the good ones are featured on www.hostelworld.com and www.hostelbookers.com.

Small Guesthouses and Bed and Breakfasts ($30 - 70pp) – The network of owner run establishments is a major of highlight of New Zealand travel. All across the country you'll find houses that have been converted into small guesthouses. Some might call them bed and breakfasts, either way, they're cute, idiosyncratic, and a cozy place to spend the night. Prices vary although this is usually equated with quality and value. Expect to pay more for little stylish touches and larger rooms. The friendly atmosphere is symbolic of the country and most guesthouse owners will provide good recommendations for onward destinations. Some guesthouses offer self catering options.

Self Catering Cottages and Mountain Huts ($30 – 100pp) – Accommodation in and around national parks often comes in the form of self catering cottages and mountain huts. On isolated hiking trails, these mountain huts can be very basic and cheap (they must be booked in advance with the national park office). At national park entrances and also in small beachside villages, the quality is much higher, although not necessarily more expensive. Note that you need to be prepared places with cottages often don't have many shops.

Hotels and Guesthouses in Major Destinations ($50 – 120pp) – Accommodation prices are ramped up in the more popular destinations and cities. There's the same commitment to boutique quality, and the focus on owner run establishments ensures quality across the board. Even a converted apartment block in Wellington offers inimitability.

Good Value Luxury Options ($80 – 200+pp) – Particularly outside the towns, New Zealand offers excellent luxury treats. Think spa retreats in the hills, private cottages perched on cliffs above the ocean, and colonial relics with roaring log fires. Thanks to low real estate prices, luxury accommodation in New Zealand can be far better value than elsewhere in the world.

Chapter 3
Immersing Yourself in New Zealand

As you might expect from a country of 30 million sheep and 4 million people, New Zealand bursts with cultural inimitability and the alternative. The blend of Maori and colonial history provides a starting point that's heightened by fun-loving free-thinking modern locals. This is a land devoid of stress and getting the most from the country necessitates a grounding in the local atmosphere. This section is about immersing yourself in the country and maximizing your experience. It provides easy tips and information that help enable the smooth transition into the land of serenity.

Take Off Your Watch and Relax

Australian pilots used to address passengers by saying, "Welcome to New Zealand, please put your watches back 20 years." Australians see the country as backward and slow. And if you're used to modern cities then there's a good chance you'll think the same. But New Zealand's very appeal lies in the relaxed and easygoing atmosphere. Every New Zealander seems to exude this unperturbed manner and unruffled smile. Rushing and stress isn't part of the local psyche and the country is all the better for it. Cramming a hundred destinations into a single day isn't going to work, nor is trying to tick attractions off a list. Take it slow, forget about the time, and you can take far more from the New Zealand experience.

Talk to Strangers

Having time to spare helps the country's famously welcoming ambiance. Strangers actually talk to each other here and meeting the locals is a regular part of the itinerary, whether that's in a bar, on a bus, or walking down the street. Particularly in a rural country, exchanging a few pleasant greetings is expected. Ignore whatever you got taught at school about not talking to strangers. If New Zealand sounds like your kind of country, the New Zealanders will be your kind of people.

The Tourist Information Office / i-Site Visitor Information Centre

New Zealand does a stellar job of marketing its attractions and destinations. Even the most rural of towns seems to have a tourist information office, sometimes combined with a Post Office, local restaurant, or farm shop. Expect a glossy layout of flyers to pick up as well as a hundred competing posters informing you of what to do. More popular destinations no longer call these centers a tourist information office. They're officially i-Site Visitor Information Centres, essentially the same thing with a fancier title. Opening hours are excellent, usually seven days from 8 / 10am until 5pm. Free maps are provided as well as detailed localized information about hiking trails. Almost without exception, these visitor's centers are a key starting point when arriving in a destination. This guidebook and the very detailed local information at the Visitor's Centre are all you need to travel New Zealand and see everything.

Get Lost

Some countries are about planning exacting itineraries and working out every meal and stop in advance. New Zealand is perhaps the antithesis. It's a place for getting lost. Firstly, it's small enough to not need a daily plan. Even a popular town like Queenstown can be walked around in ten minutes, so wandering the streets and picking a cafe by sight is easy. Local recommendations also go a long way. TripAdvisor can tell you the best ranked local restaurant. The guesthouse owner can tell you that the Fat Dog Grill does two for one lamb joints on a Wednesday night and has been a local institution for 20 years.

Secondly, such vast untamed landscapes deserve an explorer's spirit and a sense of adventure. This is truly the land of the great outdoors, and it's not the great outdoors if you're always sticking to a pre-determined itinerary. There are many other countries in the world where getting lost seems idyllic. However, New Zealand is one of the few where it's perfectly safe to do so. Despite what you might have seen at the movies, there are no strange creatures in the trees. And when you are well and truly lost, the locals will point you back on track.

Don't Litter

Few countries can rival New Zealand when it comes to pollution. There's none of it. Lakes are inspiringly clear, the air seems to delight the nostrils, and you won't find a scrap of litter anywhere. While the locals open up their country to anyone, they can't stand anyone leaving even the smallest piece of garbage behind, and yes, that includes cigarette buts. Put it in a bin. There's lots of them.

Staying Safe

Visitors to New Zealand are unlikely to encounter any crime problems. This is a country where locals still leave their doors unlocked, even when they're going out. The usual precautions apply in the cities but the crime levels here are well below those in Europe or America.

The country's reputation for adrenalin activities is well deserved. Bungee jumping, zip-lining, glacier climbing, mountain biking...New Zealand's adventure tourism industry has well-established safety procedures and it's very rare that anything happens on any organized activity. However, the wilderness can be a brutal place and misjudging personal limitations can lead to difficulties. Getting stranded on the edge of a mountain isn't a pleasant experience. Nor is heli skiing off the edge of a cliff. While it's almost impossible not to get carried away with the outdoor opportunities, taking a guide may sometimes be a sensible option. Respecting the signs about not go areas is also essential, as a few tourists found out recently when they were crushed beneath falling ice on a West Coast glacier.

Staying Healthy

When New Zealanders travel international they invariably have one major complaint; the water. The local tap water in New Zealand comes direct from glacial melts and alpine streams and it's among the cleanest in the world. It's also tasty, hence the complaints when New Zealanders travel. Buying bottled water here doesn't make any sense. Why would you when the tap water already comes straight from the source?

Healthcare and hospitals are of an excellent quality, but they are significantly spaced out. Mountain guides have direct contact with helicopter evacuation units in case of emergency. No additional immunizations are required here, other than those recommended for living in Europe or the US.

Chapter 4
An Overview of the Upcoming Chapters

This guidebook has attempted to be as practical as possible in its divide of New Zealand. Each island has been split into two and the chapters take you on a journey from the far north to the far south. This rough geographical division isn't how the locals would do it, but makes most sense for visitors coming to New Zealand. Each chapter is then sub-divided into clear routes, based on the country's state highways and available transport.

Using this approach, each of the four regions has an established entry point and base: Auckland, Wellington, Christchurch, and Queenstown. This makes it easy for incoming and outgoing transport connections. Every destination within a chapter will be within a day's ground travel of each other. Destinations are set out based on the most convenient and typical direction of travel. By following the chapter you should gather a complete idea of a potential route and itinerary for your trip. Links between regions are indicated. Here's an overview:

- **Chapter 5: Auckland and the North** – Covering the North Island as far south of Rotorua. Come here for rolling hills, beaches, bucolic landscapes, and adventures on water. It should come as no surprise that Hobbiton is set here.

- **Chapter 6: Rotorua to Wellington** – The southern half of the North Island, extensively marked by volcanic activity including mountains, geysers, and active shoots of lava. More rugged than further north but still gentle, so expect forests, vineyards, and cliffs overlooking the ocean. Three potential routes take you from north to south.

- **Chapter 7: Christchurch and the Upper South** – Starting in vibrantly rebuilt Christchurch and covering the northern half of the South Island. An eclectic and diverse land that revels in its inimitability and ability to showcase dramatic yet soothing landscapes. Two major route options, either East Coast, or across the island and West Coast.

- **Chapter 8: South of Christchurch Including Queenstown and Around** – The dramatic landscapes of the south are all about triangular peaks, glaciers, fjords, and virtually uninhabited hinterland. Come here to escape as well as find primitive natural beauty. Sometimes hard to get around but all the better for it.

Chapter 5
Auckland and the North

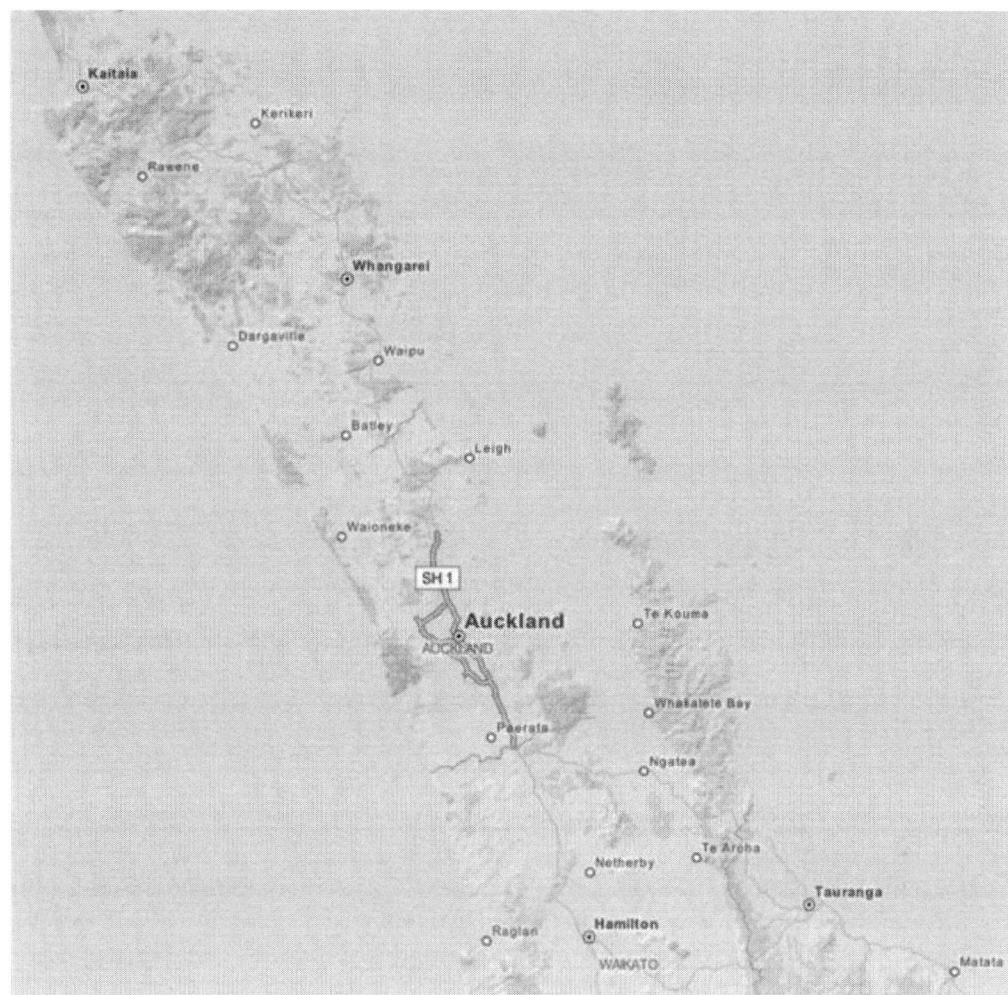

©Openstreetmap Contributors

The kaleidoscopic greenery of the North Island makes for a tranquil introduction to New Zealand's bounty. Despite being home to the country's largest city, Auckland, this region retains an unspoiled feel. Peter Jackson built Hobbiton here for precisely this reason; in the rolling hills of the north you often look around and see nothing but nature and farmland. This is the country's warmest region weather wise and a collection of long sandy beaches blend rugged New Zealand with the tropical Pacific. Outlying islands provide additional treats, as does a smattering of colonial relics and the opportunity for ocean exploration. This is a region of seemingly endless beaches, over a dozen indigenous forests, and an immersive Maori influence.

As the country's major entry point, the majority of visitors will pass through this region. Not all hang around but there's plenty of attraction for everyone that does, especially during the summer months.

Travel Essentials for Auckland and the North

Getting Here: Auckland International Airport is the main entry point into New Zealand and also has the greatest extending network of domestic flights. The Airbus Express provides direct transfers to the city center every 10 minutes from outside both domestic and international terminals. There are buses to Auckland from almost anywhere on the North Island.

Getting Around: With the largest city and national capital, there's easier and better transport options here than anywhere else in the country.

Planning an Itinerary: From Auckland the road heads either north or south and this chapter is sub-divided into these two options. Choose to head north to remote beaches and the Bay of Islands, a single road heading to the very tip of the North Island. Then you will need to return to Auckland. Alternatively, or in addition, head south and your itinerary easily links with everything in Chapter 6: Rotorua to Wellington.

Accommodation in Auckland and the North: Accommodation is generally more expensive and worse value than elsewhere in the country. There's a vast array of options. City hotels are generally favored in Auckland and Hamilton although the outlying suburbs offer something that feels more typically New Zealand (in particular, try Devonport in Auckland). Leave the cities and you'll find a strong colonial and historical flavor with converted Victorian buildings and fishing village cottages. Once you go far north, expect quaint places on the beach. Note that this region is popular with local tourism so traveling outside peak times can mean almost 50% reduction in hotel prices.

Auckland City

New Zealand's largest city still retains a quiet country backwater feel. There may be 1million people in Auckland but you can still navigate the city center easily on foot and be out in rurality within 30 minutes. Home to more boats per capita than anywhere else in the world, and regularly in the top echelons of international quality-of-life polls, Auckland is where you can find museums, fine dining restaurants, galleries, and nightlife. It's situated on a narrow peninsula that can be crossed in a day with the coast to coast walkway.

- Explore the city center on foot and you'll come across dozens of hidden surprises, from cute little restaurants to Maori art galleries and underground bars that pump until 4am. It might not sound like much of a highlight but it's practically the only place in New Zealand where you can spend a full day **exploring a city**.

- Auckland's museums offer an eclectic look at the country's history. The **Auckland War Memorial Museum** is the highlight, covering a full collection of war stories and also including exhibitions of Maori and Polynesians art.   Don't be put off by the name, this is a complete art, cultural, and natural science museum. Around the museum you'll find the **Auckland Domain park**, a chilled place to wander that houses the city's main gardens. **New Zealand's National Maritime Museum** and the Museum of Transport and Technology are also intriguing.

- Auckland offers two main adventure activities. **Climb the Auckland Harbour Bridge** for dazzling views of the cityscape, particularly in the late afternoon on a clear day. Or jump 192meters off the **Sky Tower**; it's a controlled base jump rather than a bungee jump.

- **The Sky Tower** is the highest building in the Southern Hemisphere and there's fabulous views from the top, as well as restaurants, bars, and everything else you normally find at the top of tall buildings.

- For a compelling look at art, both European and Maori influenced, try the **Auckland Art Gallery Toi o Tamaki**. It's no Louvre but it's housed in a beautiful colonial building and will also impress non art lovers.

- Spend an evening around **Auckland Harbour**, admiring the huge collection of sailing boats and sipping cocktails in one of the many ocean looking bars and restaurants. It's very lively in summer.

- For an eclectic look at the city try the **Coast to Coast Walkway**, a well-signposted walking route that crosses the city from either side of the peninsula it sits on. The walkway connects many of the main attractions and historical streets. Recommended. There's a good chance that you'll stumble upon part of the route if you're walking around town.

- Eat! Auckland has more fine dining than anywhere else in the country. Expensive, but ever popular local favorites, include **Clooney Restaurant, SidArt, One Tree Grill, Lava Dining, Cibo, Vinnies Restaurant**, and the **White Rabbit**.

- **Party!** Let's not pretend that New Zealand's party scene is cutting edge or alternative. But if you can party anywhere it's in Auckland central district.

Around Auckland

Like the rest of the country, Auckland's beauty lies in its surrounding nature. Especially in the summer months, the surrounding islands and scenic valleys provide an almost instantaneous escape into what New Zealand is so famous for. The following are all within easy day trip reach of the city and can also be incorporated into an itinerary heading to the far north of New Zealand (see the next subsection).

- Due East of the city is **Rangitoto Island**, a 600 year old volcano that's as rugged as you would expect from a volcano. It's a 45 minute ferry journey out here and then approximately one hour hike to the summit and inspiring views. Bring food, water, and suncream. You can wander around the crater rim and then trek to the lava caves.

- The same ferry to Rangitoto stops in **Devonport** (many Auckland commuter ferries also head here), a quaint fishing village with whiffs of colonial history and scents of a vibrant upcoming district. It's a good choice for accommodation if you're spending a few days in Auckland, and always a charming day out if you're not. When combining Rangitoto and Devonport, it's nicer to trek first before relaxing in the cafes of Devonport.

- Further east of Rangitoto is **Waiheke Island**, a large island that encapsulates tropical retreat with raw nature. There's long expanses of white sand to find at **Oneroa and Onetangi Beaches**, lavish rows of green **vineyards**

and wineries, and a whizz through the trees on the **flying fox zipline**. A varied and excellent day trip that would appeal to everyone.

- **Rotorua Island** offers the same picturesque scenery and beaches of the other islands. However, it was off limits to visitors for over 100 years so there's a nice feeling of being really off the beaten track.

- Arguably the pick of Auckland's nearby islands is **Tiritiri Matangi**, a tropical conservation area fluttering with colorful birds and endemic wildlife. Guided tours can explore the island but it's easy to buy a $1 map and hike unguided to hidden beaches, indigenous forest, and picturesque impressions of green. Recommended but bare in mind the NZ$70 return ferry cost from Auckland Harbour.

- The above islands are part of the **Hauraki Gulf**, a collection of 47 islands that dot the East Auckland coastline. Scheduled ferries visit the main islands but to discover the small and most untouched bays and beaches you'll need a tour – these are easily organized from the companies advertising around Auckland Harbour.

- Due north of Auckland on State Highway 1 (SH1) are the beaches of **Orewa**. Beautiful when the sun is shining but drab when the wind and rain are whipping in.

- Bristling with natural splendor and 30 minutes west of Auckland city are the **Waitakere Ranges**, an undulating expanse of mountain and forest that cascades into the ocean. Walking routes, mountain bike tracks, nature hikes, self-guided forest trails...it's a place for exploring and soaking up nature in the city. However, can be hard to reach without your own transport or booking a tour from Auckland.

The Far North of New Zealand

Leave Auckland behind and almost immediately you're into iconic countryside; mystical forests, long stretches of exposed beach, the uninhabited bliss of elsewhere in the country. This subsection runs south to north, using the N1 highway as its trunk line and then veering off to new experiences. Despite the rurality, getting public transport here is relatively easy so you don't necessarily need your own wheels, especially if you stay to the east. It's important to note that once you head north, the only way back south is to return on the same roads to Auckland.

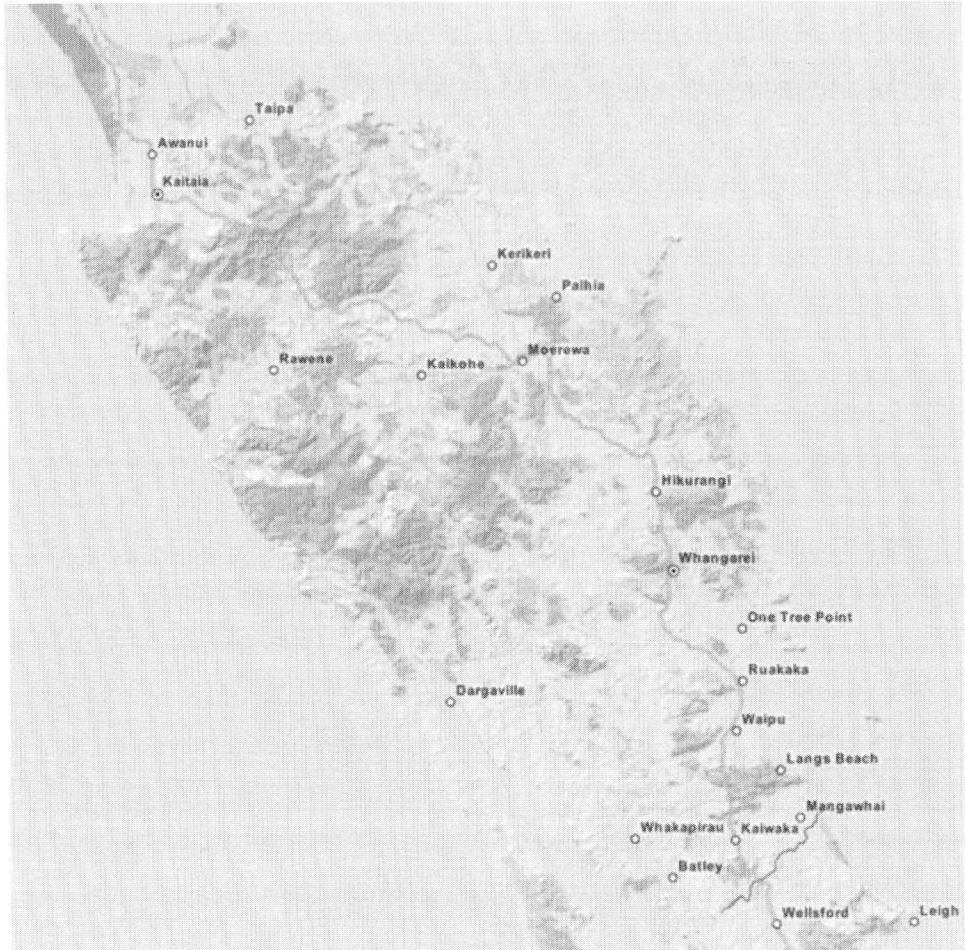
©Openstreetmap Contributors

- Combine history with a spot of kayaking in **Puhoi**, a cute village that provides the jumping off point to Wenderhold Regional Park. It's a nice lunch or coffee spot on the road going north.

- Absolutely unspoiled and bursting with primitive beauty, **Great Barrier Island** is the largest of the islands in the Hauraki Gulf. A melange of **beaches** offer white sand and good surf, there's so many **hiking trails** you don't know where to start, and the surrounding marine sanctuary offers amongst the country's best snorkeling and diving. Great Barrier Island is an idyllic escape, complete with **Kaitoke Hot Springs** and a feeling of complete immersion in nature. The downside of Great Barrier Island is the 4.5 hour ferry journey to get here. With the distance and cost it's best to commit to at least three nights here to make it worthwhile.

- Closer to shore and easy to reach using the Kawau Ferry Service from Sandspit is **Kawau Island**. Is an equally rugged concoction of sheltered bays, cute harbors, and rich Maori history.

- The rolling sand dunes and surf of **Pakiri** fulfill most preconceptions of tropical beach paradise. There's almost ten miles of white sand here and hardly a soul on it. Try a horse ride here and gallop for miles.

- Keep journeying north and you stumble upon the utopian countryside of **Matakana. Vineyards** roll onto untamed **beaches**, **scenic bays** offer prime picnic spots if you have your own vehicle, and it's famed for its local art. The **historic village center** is touristy but worth a visit, especially for the Saturday **Matakana Farmers' Market**.

- It's easy to combine Matakana with the rest of the **Tawharanui Peninsula**, barely ten minutes further north. While the beaches can feel crowded and swarming with screaming children in summer, they imbue a gentle serenity outside of peak season.

- **Whangarei** continues the theme of beaches without footprints and raw surrounding nature. **Ocean Beach** occupies a secluded bay, **Ruakaka Beach** sees few people and there's surfing to be had all year round. On a clear day, it's a short hike up **Mt Manaia** for dazzling views over these stretches of sand. Outside sunshine it might not make your itinerary, except for the stunning **Bream Head Coast Walk**, a three day hiking trail with boutique accommodation on route. **Adventure Forest** is very touristic but well organized and brimming with activities.

- As you head north, 90% of visitors stick to State Highway 1 (SH1) and the eastern coastline. With your own transport it's easy to veer off onto winding roads without vehicles and meet SH12. The forests of **Malborough**, **Waipoua**, and **Waima** can be found here, each of them virtually unexplored by other tourists. There's few facilities so bring your own supplies. Highly recommended is the Maori forest tour through Waipoua, a mystical introduction to indigenous life and the uses of the forest.

- SH1 and SH12 routes both curve inland and can join with **Wairere Boulders**, a unique concoction of massive boulders (what else?) engulfed by moss, creepers, and overhanging branches. It claims to have the largest concentrations of boulders in the world, though that's difficult to verify.

- Historic **Russell** brings a delightful radiance of charm to the north, along with evocative narratives of war and occupation. It's a popular tourist town home to lots of excellent value accommodation with views onto the Bay of Islands. Just across the bay is **Waitangi**, where the Maori chiefs and Europeans signed the Treaty of Waitangi and ensured peace in New Zealand. It's now a cute enough seaside town. Likewise **Paihia** offers views of the bay, a lot of cafes, and a tranquil place to spend a few days.

- The major attraction in Northland is the hypnotic **Bay of Islands**, a meandering expanse of deserted islets, vivid islands, and waters that swarm with dolphins. **Russell, Waitangi, and Paihia** are all equally good choices as a base for exploring the islands, offering picturesque settings and the jumping off point for marine adventure.

- Inland around the Bay of Islands are the forests of **Puketi** and **Omahuta**, the most tourist friendly and tour operated forests in the north of New Zealand. If you like easy and guided forest adventure then these are your best options. They're also the most accessible with public transport. But if the sight of wooden walkways aren't for you then just drive a little further north and west to untrammeled **Raetea, Herekina**, and **Warawara** Forests, all home toiconic Kauri trees.

- The highlight of the Bay of Islands is what can be found in the bay. Dolphins and whales regularly swim around here and **wildlife cruises** are operated by numerous operators. **Kayaking** trips and **helicopter rides** take you on journeys through and above the islets. Many tour companies offer **cruises** and **sailing** through the islets and islands, stopping at white sand beaches and quiet bays.

- Most visitors don't venture further north of the Bay of Islands area. It's practically deserted out here, although the settlements you come across are home to vibrant modern Maori culture. It's difficult to explore this section without your own transport or on a day tour from one of the Bay of

Island bases. The most popular is the **Hokianga**, a journey around the forests, villages, and dramatic geology along the Western Coastline. **Tane Mahuta** is the most visited kauri tree in the country but the photos are ruined by surrounding tourists. There are enough huge kauri trees around to not detour here.

- **Ninety Mile Beach** is the stuff of legend. Yes, it probably is around 90 miles long and once you reach the sand there's nothing but sand. This is the very far north of the North Island and the firm sand mean that most people simply take their car onto the beach and drive. Few places in the world can imbue such impressions of being lost on the edge of nowhere. It's a journey of wilderness rather than a place to sunbathe and it's important not to overestimate your hire car's ability. Day tours can also be arranged from the Bay of Islands, these last around ten hours and can be tiresome. Overnight tours are recommended.

- Across from Ninety Mile Beach is **Cape Reinga** and both are normally combined in one day. It's another evocative display of endless beach, untamed nature, and wild coastline.

South of Auckland to Rotorua

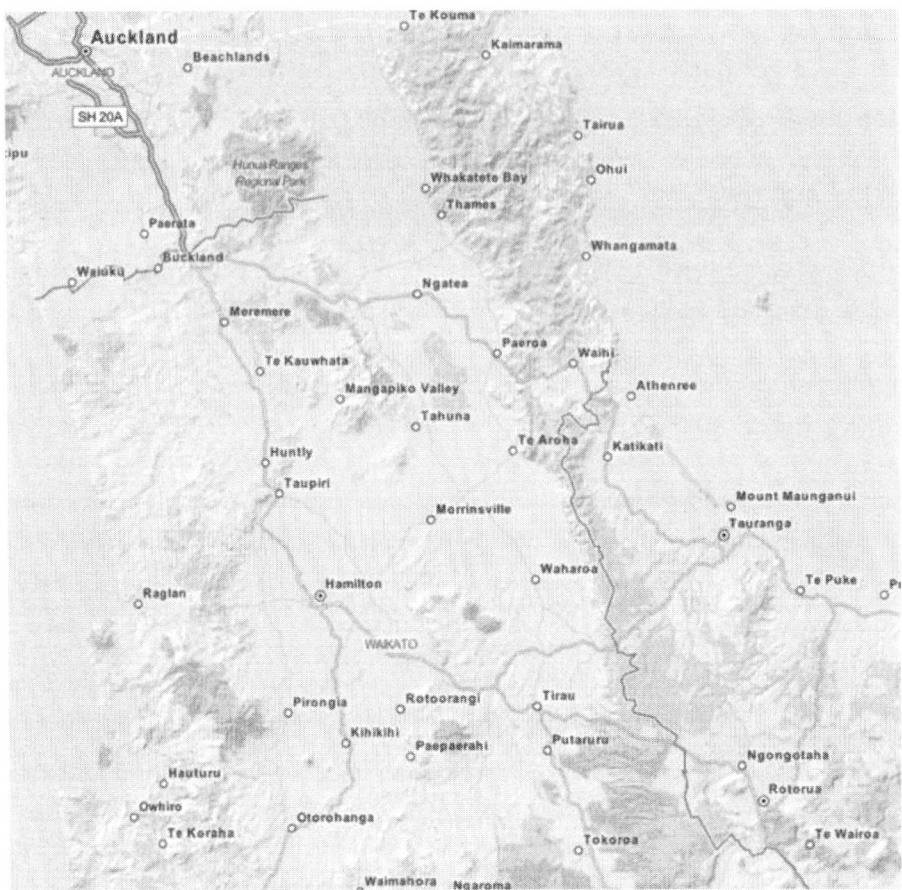
©Openstreetmap Contributors

Head South and you enter the country's most urbanized zone. A short drive on the N1 takes you to Hamilton and a weaving trail passes through green farmland to Hobbiton and then onto Rotorua. Given the kaleidoscope of experiences found north of Auckland, few people spend time in this section of the country, other than stopping at the iconic hobbit holes and moving onto Rotorua. There's still plenty to discover though, including a trek to the rim of an active volcano. This itinerary charts a route from Auckland heading south, although it's difficult to stick a single road as the attractions are dotted around. All are well accessible from Auckland by public transport.

- Excessive rainfall can be off putting but it's what makes the **Hunua Ranges** so attractive. These hills are hidden beneath a thick blanket of green and are crisscrossed by babbling rivers and flowing waterfalls. Easy to explore from the park gate and a popular spot for local tourists.

- A veering road whips out of Auckland and then doglegs up the **Awhitu Peninsula**, where you discover further displays of coastal cliffs, wild beaches, and windswept vineyards.   Not as popular as the region north of Auckland and all the better for it.

- Wonderfully named and splendidly tranquil, **Pukekohe** is a mishmash of Maori culture, colonial history, and some of New Zealand's best farm stores and food markets.

- An exhilarating and unique coastline juts out north, making for an intriguing side trip as you journey south. **Whitianga** is this peninsula's focal point and the starting point for scenic cruises and boat tours to places like Cathedral Cove and other sea caves. Towering cliffs stand proud above the boats and there's a submersive feeling of ethereal nature despite being just 30 minutes off the highway.

- **Hamilton** rarely gets seen by visitors. It's not without its charm, like the **Hamilton Gardens** and **Taitua Arboreturm**, and is one of the most peaceful cities you're ever likely to come across. However, it's short on attractions and with so much to see on the North Island it struggles to make an impression.

- More inherently attractive is **Tauranga**, nestled above the **Bay of Plenty** and a haven for everything water related. Surfing, rafting, kiteboarding, sailing, visiting the excellent **Kaiate Falls**, or simply kicking back on sunbathing. This is New Zealand's fifth largest city but it still radiates a village ambiance.

- Most visitors' Tauranga highlight is **Maunganui**. That includes wide and pristine **Maunganui Beach**, the half day hike to the summit of **Mount Maunganui**, and the easier trail that traverses the forest and coastline around **Maunganui Bluff**.

- Head further along the coast on SH2 and you reach **Whakatane**, another jumping off point for marine adventures in the Bay of Plenty, with great chances of seeing and swimming with dolphins.

- The highlight of journeys from Whakatane is **White Island**, an active bubbling hissing volcano in the heart of the bay. Tours leave from Whakatane, involving a 90 minute boat ride and then the donning of gas mask and safety equipment. Volcano reverie is all here, from stark rocky crater walls to the eery smoldering of underground gases. After trekking up and standing on the edge of an active volcano, the tour continues with a trek up the extinct cones of another. A unique and memorably New Zealand experience.

- Highlight of this region and a major attraction for the whole country is **Hobbiton**, the movie set used in Lord of the Rings and the Hobbit. It's situated on a working sheep farm, completely hidden away in volcanic green hills. Step through the gate and you enter a mythical world of 44 hobbit holes, with smoke coming from chimneys, miniature rocking chairs, and tiny flower pots. It can only be explored on a guided tour which culminates with a mug of Hobbit Stout in the Green Dragon Inn. Despite its undeniable popularity, Hobbiton is wonderfully enchanting and completely unchanged since used as a movie set. Without your own transport, tours run from Auckland and Rotorua, and it's on the hop on hop off bus routes. The cheapest day trip option is the Hobbiton bus from nearby Rotorua.

Hobbiton.

Chapter 6
Rotorua to Wellington

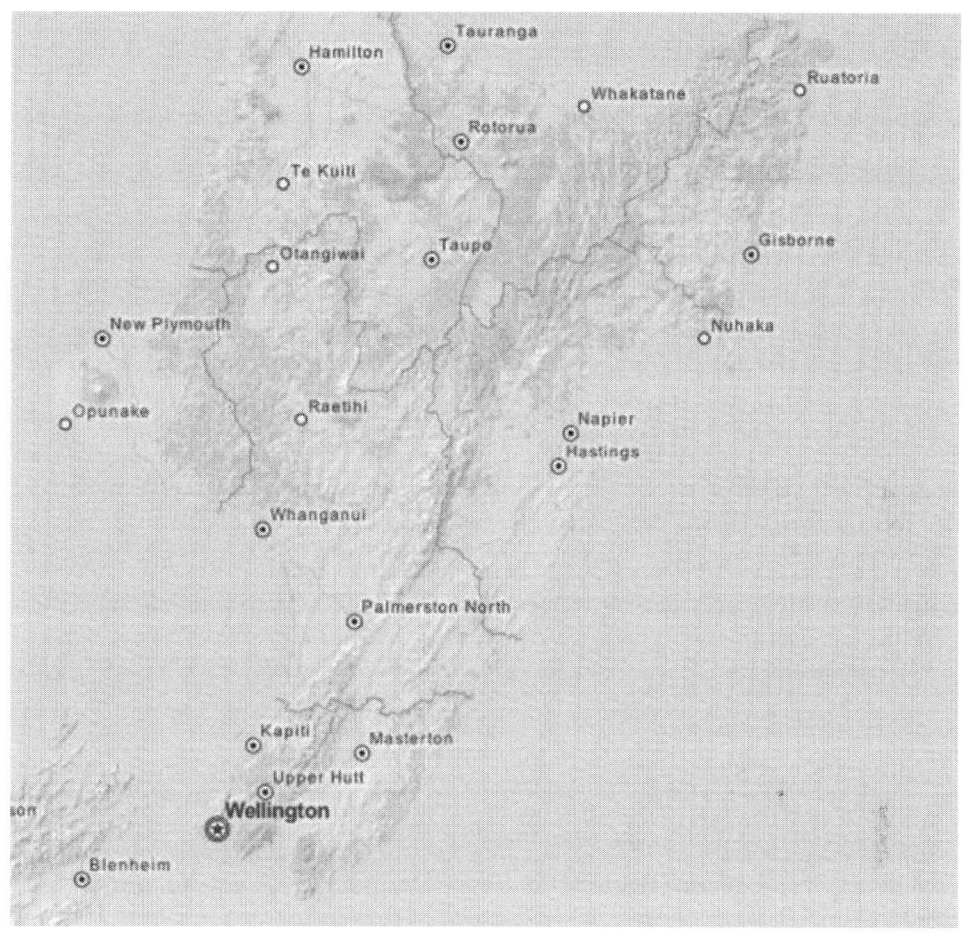

©Openstreetmap Contributors

Bristling with Maori culture and offering effervescent journeys through iconic countryside, this main part of the North Island can take weeks to fully explore. The country's volcanic past is most evident here, including exploding geysers, bubbling mud pools, and the jagged remains of domes and craters. Whereas Auckland and the far north tends to be a fair weather destination, this region can be experienced all year round. Expect to be off the beaten track most of the time, purely because the range of routes and destinations mean that few tourists stick to the same itinerary.

This section is sub-divided geographically and covers the North Island from Rotorua to Wellington, the nation's capital. These sub-sections follow the major roads and offer three distinct journeys through the North Island. SH1 and the heart of the island, SH3 and Western Coastline, and SH2 through the vineyards of Napier and the Eastern Coastline.

Travel Essentials for Rotorua to Wellington

Getting Here: A plethora of entry points are available the most common being the airports of Auckland (and then the two hour bus journey to Rotorua) and Wellington. Rotorua has a domestic airport with direct connections to Queenstown in the far south, and anyone arriving by land from the South Island will dock in Wellington.

Getting Around: This region is easier to navigate than the South Island and there's far more choice when going with public transport. Most buses and journeys take one of the state highways: SH1 (central), SH2 (east), SH3 (west) or SH4 (most direct route between Wellington and Auckland). The Wellington to Auckland train journey is a classic way to soak up the diversity of the landscape, although once you step off on route you're almost forced to wait until the next train rumbles past.

Planning an Itinerary: Many visitors use two of routes detailed in this section to form a loop starting and ending in Auckland, Rotorua, or Wellington. Others will head one way from Rotorua to Wellington using one of the routes. Challenges arise when you try to hop horizontally across the island. Visiting Napier and New Plymouth isn't particularly feasible if you're only heading one way. A more tranquil alternative is to choose one route and stick to it, the most inherently popular being to head through the heart of the island.

Accommodation from Rotorua to Wellington: This region is where the country's boutique accommodation really shines. From wine estates in Napier to mountain huts in Tongariro, or lakeside cottages in Taupo, this is where you'll find accommodation as distinctive as the setting it graces. It's predominantly good value as well. Budget lodges can be found in the many national parks and reserves, while each tiny settlement seems to feature at least a couple of converted guesthouses.

Rotorua

Bubbling with volcanic life and bursting with Maori culture, Rotorua is a well-established highlight of New Zealand. First the negatives. The geysers and sulphuric bubbles leave a faint and unpleasant whiff across town. Locals are used to it, foreigners usually arrive and wonder how the locals put up with it. Springs and geysers are exploding everywhere and the aesthetics more than compensate for the smell. Situated on a lake and surrounded by huge forests, Rotorua can keep people entertained for more than a few days, although most people stop by for a day at the thermals, a glimpse at Maori culture, and some adventure in the forest. Guesthouses and Tourist Information deserve a special mention for being able to organize and signpost people through the range of competing experiences.

- A number of villages and parks offer **Maori cultural experiences**. While these are put on for tourists, it's not like being in a zoo and pointing at the tribal people in the trees. Maoris are too proud for that to happen and the experiences do genuinely feel like a celebration of local culture. Each is set amongst a geothermal landscape and offers dancing, performing the *Haka* war dance, greetings from tribal leaders, Maori warriors looking resplendent in traditional dress, and then a meal of meat cooked on the hot stones beneath the surface. **Te Puia** is the oldest and much of the proceeds go towards promoting indigenous culture (they recently sponsored a traditional Maori canoe trip from New Zealand to Easter Island). **Tamaki Maori Village** is based in the forest and offers more of the experience you preconceive with the word Maori. **Whakarewarewa** is a third option and usually the cheapest dependent on the package you take.

- **Whakarewarewa Forest** is as mystical as they come, with towering redwoods, endless hiking trails, and hundreds of miles of mountain biking trails. Even in peak season you'll hardly see another soul once you leave the vicinity of the visitor's center.

- Rotorua exemplifies the outdoor adventure on offer in New Zealand. Choose from dozens of **hikes** in the surrounding areas, renowned **mountain bike trails, white water rafting** and dropping down the world's highest commercially raftable waterfall, as well as **kayaking** across one of the surrounding lakes. Rotorua Tourist Information has excellent and detailed information about what's available.

The geyser at Te Puia.

- Hypnotic thermals and geysers mark the whole Rotorua landscape and the best of them are housed within paid for parks. **Wai-O-Tapu Thermal Wonderland** is the most picturesque and spectacular, home to sinter terrace formations, steaming grounds, bubbling mud, and the surreal Champagne Pool. Their Lady Know Geyser explodes daily at 10.15am and it's worth the effort to make it here for the explosion. **Waimangu** offers more of the same and the guided **Geyser Link** shuttle is a good way to connect the two. **Te Puia** is the other main geothermal park, and you can get good value when combining the entrance ticket with a Maori cultural experience. The whole landscape screams of pre-historic times and their geyser explodes every couple of hours so there's less time pressure. Te Puia is also closer to the town center, only a $10 taxi ride away.

- The above thermals are certainly not for swimming. However, across the surrounding region you'll find a variety of natural **hot springs and thermal baths**. Most popular are the **Waikite Valley Thermal Pools**, but perhaps most idyllic are the **Manupirua Hot Springs**, only accessible by boat or kayak across serene **Lake Rotoiti**.

North Island West Coast Route

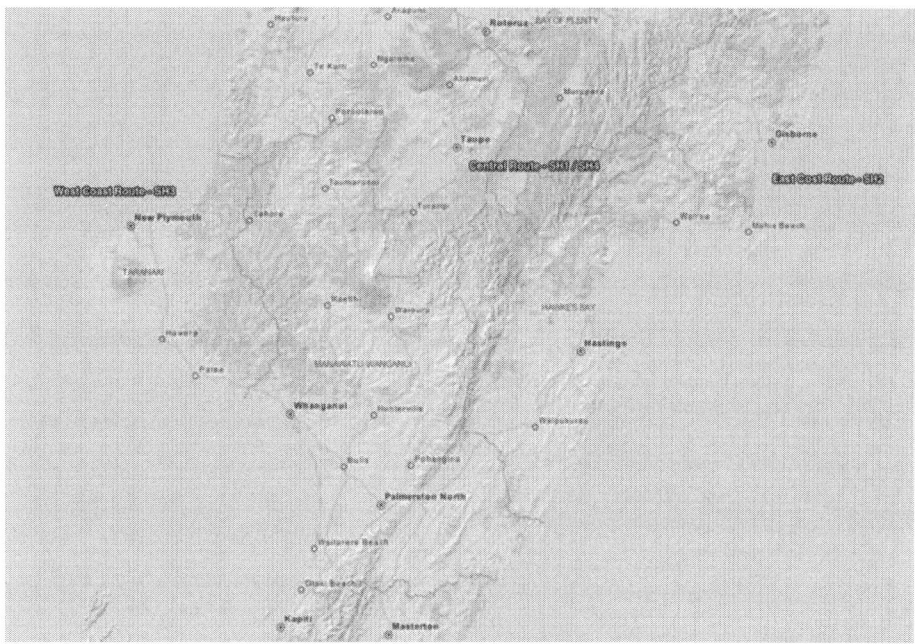

©Openstreetmap Contributors

The least visited of the North Island routes, the West Coast takes the form of iconic volcanic scenery and rough rugged coastline. It's a journey for the explorers, without the must-see attractions of elsewhere on the North but still brimming with authenticity and originality. SH3 provides a single easy connection between the destinations, running from Hamilton and then adjacent to the coastline until it joins SH1 at Palmerston North near Wellington. To join this road from Rotorua, the easiest routes are to head directly west and meet SH3 by Waitamu and its caves, or to take a winding road west from Lake Taupo. Taking this route provides a treat in off the beaten track New Zealand and can be done in one day or a week. The following experiences are listed north to south.

- The **Waitomo Caves** seem to epitomize New Zealand's enhancement of nature. Huge caverns and labyrinthine caves stretch for miles through the Waitomo area. On one hand they offer memorable journeys through geology, in particular the **Spellbound Glowworm and Caves Tours** and the **Raukuri Caves and Bush Scenic Reserve.** But these are also places of adventure, like abseiling 100 meters into canyon, jumping into underground rivers, climbing over slippery rock, and heading miles into eerie darkness. **Waitomo Adventures** are the longstanding tour operator guiding the journey. Another option is to raft in the caves, so called black water rafting by the **Legendary Black Water Rafting Co**.

- From Waitomo, SH3 takes a direct and remote route along craggy coastline and thick green forest. It's a beautiful journey with many deserted spots for a picnic and rest. Pass through **Mokau** where **scenic boat cruises** are available then **Urenie**, before meeting the major town in this area, **New Plymouth**.

- **Mount Taraniki** looms over New Plymouth and this stretch of coast, an often snow sprinkled and precarious summit providing the iconic backdrop to most of your photos. It's a tough and tricky 6-8 hour return hike to the top, with the diehards setting off at 2am to arrive for sunrise views. Mount Taraniki kills more than any other New Zealand mountain so come prepared. However, around the foothills there's a wonderful array of **family friendly walking trails and hikes**, everything from 30 minutes to four hours. The Visitor's Centre is an an excellent first port of call.

- A broad boulder strewn promenade stretches 4-5 miles through New Plymouth and the surrounding beaches and bays. The **Coastal Walkway** makes for a more gentle alternative if you're looking for a scenic walk and don't like the look of the volcanic slopes. Go at low tide and you can also wander onto the beaches.

- New Plymouth has a number of old buildings and reminders of its fishing industry are all around. However, it's recently found fame in New Zealand for its parks and gardens. **Pukekura Park, Pukeiti Rhododendron Park, Tupare Park**, and **Kawaroa Park**, are all excellent examples of their originality and ability to offer omnipresent festivals of green in the town.

- From New Plymouth SH3 skirts inland, heading east of Taranaki to the old settlement of Stratford. The town's nearby forests evoke impressions of a lost world, although the name **Goblin Forest** already imbue ideas before you arrive. Stratford is the also the southern end of the **Forgotten World Highway** (see North Island Central Route).

- After joining the coast again at **Hawera**, another town majestically framed by Mount Taraniki, you pass through **Whanganui**, a popular destination for families with its parks, lake, and gentle river adventures. Keep heading south and the road meets the N1 (see North of Wellington below).

North Island Central Route

Heading due south from Rotorua provides an immersion in mystical and mythical scenery. SH1 and SH4 cut through the mountains, rolling into the kind of Middle Earth that lives in visitor's preconceptions. There's skiing to be found in winter, the serenity of Lake Taupo, a couple of high volcanic peaks, and an array of tiny villages. As always, there's plenty of forest adventure to be had as well. This route is most popular with anyone with a penchant for excitement and the outdoors, and being central means there's the possibility of combining the journey with destinations on the east or west. The following experiences are listed north to south.

- Note that a number of the thermal and Maori attractions listed under Rotorua, are situated south of the town on the road to Taupo. With your own transport you can stop at **Tamaki, Waikiti Valley**, and **Wai-O-Tapu** on route.

- Keep heading south and halfway between Rotorua and Taupo is **Orakei Korako Cave and Thermal Park**. With its geysers, mud pools, and flowing silica terraces, Orakei is as impressive as the thermal parks closer to Rotorua. It's an excellent choice for those short on time as it provides an inspiring look at the thermals without having to stop in Rotorua. For those on public transport it's an easy half day trip from Taupo.

- Placid **Lake Taupo** hides an explosive past. The tranquil waters fill the caldera of one of the planet's biggest super volcanoes, and they're popular for trout fishing, lazy boat trips, and long days walking or biking around the shore. **Taupo** town itself is also quiet and calm, making the area a popular destination for anyone with a few weeks to spare. Note that Taupo has its own airport and makes an alternative entry point to flying to Rotorua.

- The majority of attractions lie north of the lake around the town. These include the rapids of **Huka Falls**, the **Aratiatia Rapids**, and **Spa Thermal Park**. If you don't want to get wet, there's also the indoor 4D virtual white water rafting rides at **White Water World Taupo**. As with most things

New Zealand there's weeks of adrenalin and relaxation to fill the time; **skydiving, jet boating across the river, Lake Taupo kayaking**, and a **dozen sailing experiences**.

- SH1 heads along the western side of the lake to Turangi on its southern shore, one of New Zealand's most popular **white water rafting** destinations. With **Mount Ngauruhoe** (hike or take a ski lift to the top for stunning lake views) gazing down, and rivers that gush through virgin forest, there's over 60 individual rapids to negotiate.

- Those with their own transport can head west from Turangi to **Taumarunui.** This is the northern start of the **Forgotten World Highway**, a dramatic and challenging road that cuts through remote **Whanganui National Park**, the **Waitotara Forest**, and on to Stratford. Four wheel drive is recommended if it's been raining heavily as there's a tricky eight mile off road section near the **Bridge to Nowhere** to negotiate. Tour companies also offer day trips along this road. For off the beaten track New Zealand and rolling through surreal landscapes, this is one of the country's premier experiences. However, it's not an easy road and it's a long day. Splitting it up with an overnight stop in the national park is another option.

- The North Central Route is the one taken by the **Wellington to Auckland Northern Explorer rail line**, a slow thrice weekly trip that traverses almost the full length of the North Island. While the route is different to that of the Forgotten World Highway (see above), the scenery is equally impressive and primitive. Without doing the full Wellington to Hamilton / Auckland in one stretch the options are limited. Either spend two days **National Park,** beside Mount Tongariro (see below) or alight at National Park and catch a local bus towards Rotorua.

- South of Turangi the road splits, snow dappled **Tongariro** providing the geographical barrier. SH1 is more direct and goes east, while SH47 joins SH4 on the east. **Tongariro National Park** provides a domineering sight, a series of perfect domes cascading down into gentle green slopes. The most common entry point for activities and hiking trails here are via the HS4 route. During winter it offers excellent skiing at the **Whakapapa Ski Resort**, and during summer the ski lifts are still in operation to take visitors to the summit for glorious views.

- Around its fringes, Tongariro is easy to explore, with **hiking, rafting, biking, horse trails, and quad biking**. But the high precipitous peaks can be inaccessible (the ski lift aside). **Scenic flights** cruise over the peaks of Tongariro, Ngauruhoe, and Ruapehu, as well as the vibrant caldera lakes hidden in the park. Otherwise, atmospheric **multi day hiking trails** connect the peaks with accommodation in mountain huts on route. With the volcanoes still emitting smoke it does feel very much like walking through Mordor. For a single summit climb, **Ruapehu** is the most accessible. Despite the beauty, Tongariro isn't overly popular and on almost any trail you're lost in its silence and primitive majesty.

- South of Tongariro most people make a direct beeline south for Palmerston North and then Wellington. Although, in this part of the world, direct means meandering through forests and hills and nothing ever being straight. To continue this route see North of Wellington below.

North Island East Coast Route

Ah, the East Coast. Quiet countryside, rolling vineyards, and an elegant journey through soporific landscapes. Maori influence is strong here, as is the tranquil atmosphere that has everyone taking off their watch and throwing the diary out of the window. Destinations can be remote and they're all the better for it, the immersion in rural New Zealand epitomized by a journey that takes State Highway 2 (SH2). From Rotorua or anywhere in the North, the road first hits Whakatane and the Bay of Plenty (see chapter 5) before veering through the forests to Gisborn and making a mellow coastal journey south. The following experiences are listed north to south.

- Leaving Rotorua or Whakatane and taking SH2, there's little on route until you reach **Gisborn** on the eastern coastline. Those with their own transport can completely follow the coast by first taking SH35, although this is a lonely and rarely seen part of New Zealand.

- **Gisborn** is a cute settlement framed by Pacific Ocean rollers and wineries. Long white water waves make **surfing lessons** popular here and the water is surprisingly warm. These waters also bring marine delight and some excellent **scuba diving**, with the strong possibilities of seeing some of the smaller shark species. While the **vineyards** aren't as well known as those further south in Hawkes Bay, they still offer a good afternoon of tasting and elegant views.

- With farmyards and tractors abound SH2 heads south into the **Hawkes Bay region**, renowned for its wineries and flat fertile landscapes. This was one of the first areas to to be colonized and continues to preserve stereotypes about New Zealand being a land of too many sheep.

- Napier tends to be the most popular base in the Hawkes Bay region. It's a quaint old town, stuffed full of art deco furniture (check out the **Art Deco Trust**) and surrounded by wineries. The chief attractions are **wine tasting** and **wine tours**. A dozen companies offer days out that take in four or five wine estates and inclusive tasting. This is one of New Zealand's most famous wine regions and home to a number of wineries that have garnered international acclaim. Complimenting the wine, Napier has some excellent **organic restaurants**. Most people prefer to stay in Napier than the adjacent and more developed Hastings.

- Outside wine tasting and food, Napier's attractions are somewhat spurious, created for those who stay in town for more than a couple of days. There's a **vintage car museum, farm experience, water park**, and some nice **coastal walks**. More bizarre, and certainly more raucous, **Cape Kidnappers** (yes, that's a real name) is home to the world's largest gannet collection, the big white birds filling a whole beach with their antics. For views of the town and bay, it's a relatively easy two hour hike up **Te Mata Peak**.

- The **tiny towns** that dot the roads in Hawkes Bay vociferously scream of **rural farming communities**. It often feels like a journey back in time although it's hard to stop at them without your own transport. There's no obvious highlights but it's impossible not to find a cute guesthouse, homestead, pub, or country restaurant. It's just over an hour from Napier to Palmerston North.

- One favorite photo spot is the sign for **Taumatawhakatangihangakoauauotamateaturipukakapikimaungahoronukupokaiwhenuakitanatahu,** a far from spectacular green hill that's in the Guinness World Records for having the longest place name.

- The cliffs and beaches on the Southern Hawkes Bay coastline are generally reserved for **exclusive farm retreats and lodges**. Again, they're difficult to reach without your own wheels.

North of Wellington

Each of the three routes converge around Palmerston North as the North Island narrows into a peninsula, around one hour north of Wellington. Almost everyone will pass through this region coming from the north, and few people stop on route. These attractions are also within easy day trip reach of Wellington for those arriving directly in the nation's capital.

- **Palmerston North** is an endearing enough town with old colonial streets and a smattering of museums. Few linger though as Wellington offers more far more.

- Most of the attractions lie on SH1 and the western piece of the peninsula. The exception to this are the **historic towns** on SH2, each of them doused in 200 years of history and providing an ambient journey into the time of the first settlers. **Masterton, Carterton, Greytown, Featherston** can all be explored in half a day and there's a collection of good **vineyards** in the vicinity.

- Barely 20 minutes north of Wellington there's a forested coastline which isn't really for sunbathing. Large collections of fur seals hang out on the rocks although you'll need a **private seal safari** to see them as it's mostly on private land. Fringed by forested mountains, this coastline provides panoramic views over Cook Strait and a number of towns that mix Maori and colonial history; the **Kapiti Coast** is the most enchanting, accessible by train or bus. In particular, this is a place for **sunset views with a packet of fish and chips**. Paraparaumu and Otaki are where this can be best realized.

Wellington

Windy Wellington is among the world's most gentle capitals. Despite the line of modern buildings along the harbor, the atmosphere is more of country village than bustling hub. Most appealing is its size. In just a couple of days you can soak up boutique city life and the abundance of nature and vineyards on its doorstep. A central location and excellent transport connections mean that many visitors stop in Wellington during their trip.

Recreating Lord of the Rings on a movie location tour.

Wellington is where large **movie production centers** are based. Hundreds of movies are filmed in New Zealand and the Wellington studios were used for Avator, Lord or the Rings, District 9, and more. **Lord of the Rings location tours** reveal exactly what their name promises, and the **Weta Cave** mini-museum shows how the special effects are applied.

- Gasp at the windy city from the air by climbing up **Mount Victoria**. You can also drive to the top if you don't fancy the ascent through the forest.

- Unquestionably New Zealand's finest museum, **Te Papa Tongarewa** (or the Museum of New Zealand to use its English title) offers an all-encompassing, honest, and interactive look at the country's history. It's also free.

- Te Papa holds center stage on the **Wellington Waterfront**, an endearing place of boats setting sail and bars serving sundowners.

- For an ongoing narrative of cafes, parks, sculptures, and coastline, walk from the **waterfront to Oriental Bay**.

- The city is justifiably proud of its **restaurants and cafes**, the majority of them utilizing the fertile surrounding slopes for all their wine, coffee, and organic food. Local seafood is almost always good, epitomized by the **Ortega Fish Shack**. Fine dining options favored by locals include **Logan-Brown, Muse on allen, Hippopotamus**, and **The Larder**.

- Get around the city on the historic **Wellington Cable Car**, a slow but captivating trip from Lambton Quay to the lookout at Kelburn.

- **Cuba Street** is the city's slightly fabricated attempt at bohemia and being hip. It's entertaining and cool, although you can't help thinking that Wellington doesn't need to try and be colorfully trendy. There's enough coolness to not warrant the replica of artistic European capital suburbs.

- **Wellington's Heritage Precinct** features unique remains from colonial times, quirky stories seeming to radiate from the stained glass and old wooden structures. Wandering around here is always an experience, the highlight being a trip to **Old St Paul's** the exquisite gothic wooden cathedral.

Chapter 7
Christchurch and the Upper South

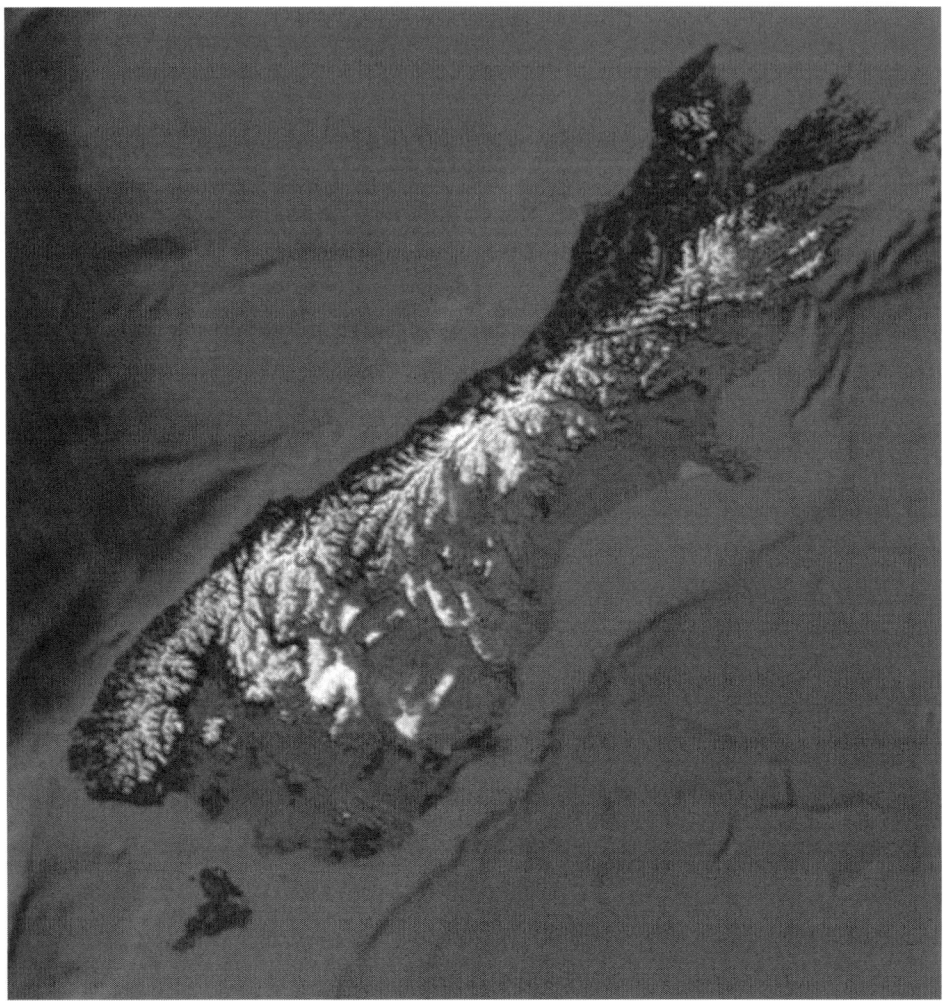

This aerial gives an idea of the South Island's topography, the snow capped mountain chain separating West Coast from fertile East Coast.
©openstreetmap contributors.

Decimated by earthquake yet rebuilt with enthusiasm and ingenuity, Christchurch symbolizes the unique beauty of the upper South. An eclectic mix of landscapes provide the starting point, from the views of the Southern Alps twinkling in the distance, to golden beaches, vineyards, and serene national parks. Christchurch and the Upper South has a little bit of everything, an almost all-encompassing snapshot of what New Zealand has to offer. Tourism is well developed here and it can sometimes feel busy in peak season. Because while this region contains a bit of everything, visitors tend to stick to a wine tour, Abel Tasman National Park, Marlborough Sounds, and a couple of days in Blenheim or Nelson.

This chapter splits the region into five distinct sub-sections, starting with Christchurch and culminating with Tasman Marlborough in the north. Most visitors will then likely choose one route between them, SH1 or SH6.

Getting Here: Christchurch is the obvious aerial entry point and has a busy international airport. A regular bus travels from outside arrivals to downtown. If arriving by boat from the North Island then you'll land in Picton (see Tasman-Marlborough). When arriving from the far south (see chapter 8) there are two distinct routes. Either SH1 along the eastern coastline to Christchurch, or SH6 along the West Coast to Greymouth.

Getting Around: While the route options are limited, the choice of public transport is generally good and there is little advantage of your own transport, particularly when compared to other regions. As well as the buses and hop on hop off services, two sublime train lines provide scenic enchantment; Christchurch to Picton (and connections with the North Island ferry) and Christchurch to Greymouth.

Planning an Itinerary: From Christchurch visitors have essentially two choices for routes into Tasman Marlborough and the Upper South. The quickest is the SH1 along the East Coast to Blenheim and Picton. Alternatively, explore Canterbury and then cross east to west before heading north to Tasman Marlborough.

Accommodation in Christchurch and the Upper South: While the earthquake wiped out many hotels in Christchurch's central district, the city's accommodation standard doesn't seem to have deteriorated. A sprinkling of smaller guesthouses have sprung up and that's true of the whole region. This is a region where it pays to go for the small and local, New Zealand's regal hospitality in full show.

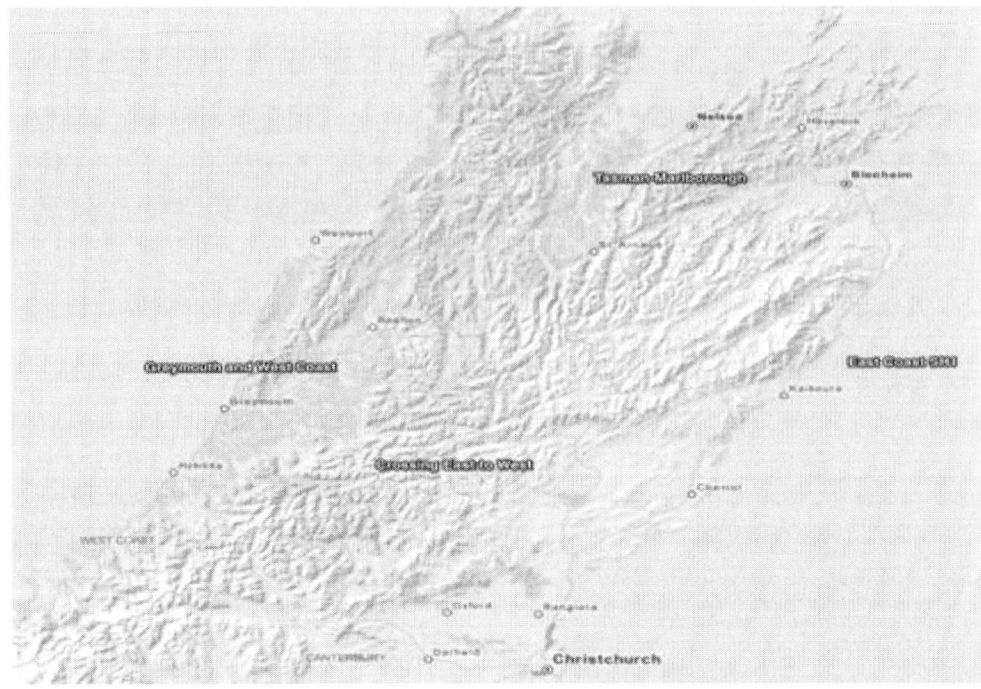

©openstreetmap contributors

Christchurch

New Zealand sits on a fault line of fire. The undercurrent of activity has created so many of the country's renowned sights, from jagged mountains to active craters and exploding geysers. This fault line tragically ripped through Christchurch, the 2011 earthquake leaving half the city in ruins and claiming 185 lives. You would expect a downtrodden depressed city. Except Christchurch is buoyant and enthusiastic, the locals finding creative solutions and rebuilding the streets. It's become a remarkable ode to the potential spirit and togetherness of a city.

- **Soaking up the atmosphere** is the essential Christchurch experience. Don't expect glum faces and laments for the past. Instead, the city is about positivity and looking forward.

- **185 Empty White Chairs** is the city's earthquake memorial, and **Victoria Park** is a good example of the double quick regeneration since. A deeper narrative of events since 2011 is provided at **Quake City**, an excellent and informative retelling of pre, during, and post disaster. **Canterbury Ca-**

thedral is now in ruins and it's been replaced by **Cardboard Cathedral;** both are other good free to visit landmarks in the city.

- Like all New Zealand cities, Christchurch is framed by greenery and majestic surroundings. For views across the city and the Canterbury Plains take the **Christchurch Gondola** up **Port Hills**; there are distant views of the Southern Alps on a clear day. Port Hills is worth exploring, both for its aching **ocean views** and easy to follow **historic walking trails**.

- Christchurch is green. The **Botanic Gardens** combine endemic and exotic plants as does **Mona Vale**, just outside the city. Cutting a slice through the city is the **Avon River**, a good place for a stroll and coffee. Keep on this river and you reach the **Riccarton House and Bush**, an opulent colonial building tucked away in native bush forest.

- Not everything was lost in the earthquake. Colonial and ancient heritage is still alive, particularly via the hop on hop off **Christchurch Tramway**, an excellent way to get around the city.

- In summer, a few nearby beaches become popular with the locals, including the bays of the **Banks Peninsula** and **Waimairi Beach**. The former is popular all year round with hikers, as is the **Godley Head**, a coastal walk heading out in the other direction.

- Charming **Akaroa** is the jumping off point for marine adventures around the peninsula. Dolphins patrol these waters, as do seals and occasionally migratory whales. **Sailing cruises** are wonderful when the weather shines, as are **guided kayak trips** through waters that fill an extinct volcanic crater. On land, **The Giant's House** in Akaaroa forms a utopian mix of mosaics, colors, and opulent interiors. It's worth the entry ticket and remains one of the country's most intriguing buildings.

SH1 and the East Coast to Picton

SH1 heads directly up the East Coast, passing through a series of vineyards and Blenheim before arriving at Picton In little over two hours. Those short on time are likely to take this route. With public transport few people stop other than at Blenheim, but there are a couple of intriguing places on route.

- Barely 30 minutes outside Christchurch, the **vineyards of Waipara** are a popular day trip and the first stopping point when heading north. Guided tours can be organized from Christchurch and almost a dozen wineries offer tasting, with a couple offering **wine discovery tours – Torlesse Wines** is recommended for this. Vineyards continue to dot the landscape as you head further north and it's sometimes hard to resist a five minute detour for another tasting.

- **Kaikoura's** attractions are those that lie off-shore, the **abundant marine life** enticing many visitors. A melange of sperm whales, dolphins, killer whales, and seals, can all be encountered on **wildlife cruises**. They're so abundant that Whale Watch offer a 80% refund if you don't see a giant sperm whale. Many operators now offer **swimming with dolphins and seals** in their natural environment. Kayaking and scenic flights provide new angles and fishing charters are popular. There's a profuseness of competing tour companies and the **Kaikoura Visitor Centre** makes a good non-biased starting point to get your head around everything on offer. Just north of Kaikoura the **Ohau Waterfall Walk and Seal Pups** is a cheaper way to see the marine life, but the seals are not around in summer.

- There's little but farmland until you rumble into **Blenheim**, an artisan meets agriculture town that will appeal to all wine lovers and foodies. Over 20 wineries are within easy driving distance and over a dozen tour companies ensure that someone else does the driving with a **Marlborough wine tour.** A guided or self-guided **wine bike tour** can visit over ten vineyards, just don't join the daily casualties riding their bikes into a farm fence. With its range of **organic restaurants** and good hotels, Blenheim tends to attract older tourists.

- **Picton** marks the end of the road, both for the SH1 and those coming on the SH6. Few people spend the night here, most preferring to jump straight on the ferry to the North Island. A series of sounds provide an evocative background to the town, with almost a fifth of New Zealand's total coastline found here.

- Numerous companies offer cruises and boating safaris onto these **Marlborough Sounds**, with tranquil stops in secluded bays and numerous bush-covered ridge lines. Note that the ferry traverses through these sound so if crossing to the North Island the value in also taking a Marlborough cruise is debatable. Still, when the weather is good, the Marlborough Sounds provide journeys into untouched native forest and bays dancing with dolphin fins.

- Adventurous souls may be interested in the **Queen Charlotte Track** along the perimeter of the sounds, a three to five day journey made of walking, mountain biking, or kayaking.

Canterbury and Crossing East to West

A seemingly impenetrable line of mountains carve through the South Island, separating the valleys and farmland of the east with the rough coastline of the west. To cross east to west there are three viable options, each a spectacular journey across untrammeled landscapes and over a long mountain pass. The first is the SH8 to Mount Cook National Park and then onwards to Queenstown and the far south (see chapter 8). The two northern routes meet with the SH6 on the West Coast and are detailed here. Both routes can join with Greymouth, the jumping off point for the West Coast National Parks (also see chapter 8), or can be used to head north into Tasman-Marlborough.

East to West on SH73

This route passes through Arthur's Pass National Park and a number of winter ski resorts, crisscrossing over rivers and valleys before joining SH6 halfway between Greymouth and Hokitika. It's three hours driving time in good conditions but allow close to five given the number of viewpoints on route. Attractions are listed east to west.

- For a slow and gentle immersion in the scenic changes and dazzling mountain pass, take the **Christchurch to Greymouth railway line**. Few world train journeys are as picturesque, and it's far more enchanting (and more expensive) than the equivalent bus.

- With the mountains on one side, the coastline on the other, and the green Canterbury plains in between, **hot air ballooning above Canterbury** provides an aesthetic wonderland for a hefty price tag. Can be booked in Christchurch; based on SH73 just outside the city.

- Heading west you pass through the **Mount Cheeseman ski area** and **Korowai-Torlesse Tussocklands Park**, where **Lake Lyndon** makes for an impressive picnic and viewpoint stop. Mountains start to surround the road, the peaks of **Enys** and **Castle Hill** domineering from alternate sides. There are no settlements around here, although **mountain bike tracks** and **hiking trails** abound. All are well signposted from the road.

- Pass **Craigieburn Forest Park**, the **Waimakariri River**, and then cut through the heart of Arthur's Pass National Park. The eponymous pass is the highlight of the journey and you're deeply submerged by mountains that tower down from 360 degrees. **Arthur's Pass Visitor Centre** provides detailed information on the remote adventures to have and accommodation is dotted along the road. In winter, the **Temple Basin Ski Area** is actually a famed destination for snowboarders, with halfpipes, jumps, and many sections for showing off. In summer, this is the easiest spot for **half day hikes** with all-encompassing views.

- SH73 keeps weaving as you tick off the mountains: **Wilson, Rolleston, Temple, Franklin, Scarface, Alexander**, then **Treacy** and **Turiwhate** as the road descends towards the West Coast, passing the Kapitea Reservoir on route. In summer it's possible to detour north to ultra secluded Lake Poerua and Lake Brunner.

East to West on SH7

After following SH1 out of Christchurch, SH7 provides the most northerly crossing of the mountains. While not as spectacular as the SH73, it's still an achingly authentic journey through forests, mountains, and valleys dappled with lakes. This won't be an option without your own transport. The advantage is the northern routing which provides easy access to Tasman-Marlborough and Nelson Lakes National Park.

- Adrenalin fueled adventures put Hanmer Springs on the map, the tourist centered town reveling in its offering of **white water rafting, bungee jumping, quad biking**, and then a couple of **spas** to counteract the adrenalin. It's good, but not as spectacular as what's on offer further south.

- Just before **Victoria Forest Park** the road splits, with SH65 heading straight into Tasman-Marlborough. This is the quickest inland route north, joining SH6 and Murchison.

- **Reefton** is just about the only settlement of more than 50 people, located after Victoria Forest Park. The park offers a number of mountain bike and hiking trails although they're not as impressive as those in Arthur's Pass. From Reefton, either head north to hit Tasman-Marlborough or continue on SH7 all the way to Greymouth.

Greymouth and the West Coast

Tiny Greymouth provides the base of this section as it's a strategic crossroads for many journeys in the North Island. SH73 and SH7 meet the West Coast SH6 here. You're likely to pass through here when visiting the West Coast National Parks (see chapter 8) and when journeying the length of the South Island. But this is far more than a transit point. With mountains cascading into ocean and a green canopy all around, this is an extraordinary landscape that often has people extending their stay from days to weeks. The destinations and experiences here are listed from south to north.

- **Hokitika's coastline** come straight from a post apocalyptic movie, all bumpy and strange. Delve into **Glow Worm Dell**, easily as good as other natural glow worm caves in the country but free and explorable without a guide. Wander through **Hokitika Gorge Scenic Reserve** (also free) for shimmering blue waters and endemic forest, and / or take a **jet boat** along the Hokitika River.

- **Greymouth's** dazzling surrounds make it a quaint place to break up a journey. Check out the **Monteith's Brewing Company tour** if you've been craving a day on the beer. It's a surprisingly small town with the main attractions being adventures in nearby **Omotumotu Scenic Reserve** and **Rapahoe Range Scenic Reserve**. Think **quad bikes, horse rides, hikes, biking**; detailed information from the visitor's centre. **West Coast Wilderness Trail** is particularly recommended.

- Mining provides Greytown's history, first gold and now coal. **Shantytown** attempts to recreate the mid 19th century times although it feels a little fake. **Brunner Mine Site Walk** is a more authentic look into life in the mines, and **Dragon's Cave rafting** is an actual adventure in the caves.

- SH6 north from Greytown passes huge swathes of beach and there's a couple of cute accommodation options for anyone seeking pure escapism. **Punakaiki** is a tiny community with a dramatic attraction, **Pancake Rocks**. A series of towering rock pinnacles stand alone in the ocean, battered by the surf and resembling a mythical giant's fingers. It's a hugely popular stopping point with oodles of tourists. But it's worth a place in any itinerary.

- Continuing further north, with the forested mountains of **Paparoa National Park** as the backdrop, there are a couple of attractions for anyone self driving; **cave rafting in Charleston** and the **coal museum in Westport**. SH6 now heads eastwards and into Tasman-Marlborough. Note that a passable road continues up the West Coast from Westport but it terminates in Karamea – these is no route through to Abel Tasman National Park and the northwest peninsula.

Tasman-Marlborough and the Upper South

One of New Zealand's most romantic destinations, Tasman-Marlborough is framed by huge swathes of vineyards, cute old towns, and further adventures into surrounding national parks. It's at somewhat of a visual crossroads, the mountains slipping from the west and joining the rolling landscapes of the east. Wine isn;t the only treat the tickles the senses, Tasman-Marlborough continues New Zealand's tradition of adventurous activity, albeit with a more upmarket feel. Whereas younger travelers tend to find utopia in Queenstown, Tasman-Marlborough seems to be the preferred long stay destination for older visitors wanting natural beauty and serenity with all the modern amenities. Destinations here are listed south to north.

- As SH6 rolls north and joins SH65 (see Canterbury and Crossing East to West), **Murchison** and the **Buller River** makes for a popular overnight stop. The **jet boating** here rivals that of anywhere in the country, with 55mph races along pink granite canyons, and **white water rafting** that's best when the rivers are high in spring.

- Bursting with primitive splendor and generally off the tourist radar, **Nelson Lakes National Park** is a prime hiker's and camper's playground. **Lake Rotoiti** is the easy choice for gaping panoramas without having to hike.

Further afield there are **looped walks** to various lakes and **multi-day traverses** with accommodation in based mountain huts. **St Arnaud** is the gateway village for accessing the national park and there's good accommodation on offer.

- Indelibly artistic and buzzing with energy, **Nelson** is perhaps New Zealand's funkiest town. Many use it as a base to explore the whole Tasman-Marlborough region, with the concoction of **boutique hotels** a particular highlight. Local tour companies offer trips to everywhere in the region and it's impossible to miss their adverts in the center of town.

- With a wine and cafe culture, time moves slowly in Nelson. **The World of WearableArt and Classic Cars Museum** is a local institution and an almost must-see, made even better with a few glasses of local red beforehand. Elsewhere in town you'll find well preserved **Broadgreen Historic House**, a collection of **gardens**, and the leftovers from colonial times at **Founders Park**.

- East of Nelson is the region of **Marlborough**, New Zealand's largest wine growing region. See also SH1 and the East Coast to Picton for more information. Wine is the obvious attraction with dozens of **award winning wineries**, including major international exporters. Most New Zealand wine you find around the world originates here and numerous tour companies offer trips from Nelson and Blenheim. The mystical Marlborough Sounds extend along the coastline and it's a stunning journey by **foot or road from Nelson to Blenheim**. Boat cruises onto the **Pelorus Sounds** start in **Havelock**; these are less touristic but equally enchanting as those from Picton further east.

- You've now reached the northern coastline, so peer out onto **Tasman Bay** and soak up the ocean rollers. Between Nelson and Motueka is a stretch of **golden sand beaches** and cottage accommodation. From both towns you can organize marine adventures and trips into Abel Tasman National Park. Kayaking is good here with trips across the water to a marine reserve.

- Vibrantly green and full of surprise, **Abel Tasman National Park** is one of New Zealand's major destinations. Its popularity comes from the range of **golden beaches** almost completely without footprints, and the complete lack of roads. Many visitors come on **easy day trips** to check out the beaches, the thick green awning providing an almost tropical backdrop to the ocean waters. **Boat cruise** companies depart from Marahau and Kaiteriteri with stops at numerous beaches. Note that there are no shops or services in the park so you have to bring everything with you and then take it all away.

- Further marine adventure can be found at **Tonga Island Marine Reserve**, accessible via a long kayak or a hike from Tonga Quarry. Arguably the finest inland adventure is a **canyoning trip** arranged from Marahau; abseil, jump, slide, and traverse a river deep in the forest.

- Abel Tasman offers a selection of **multi-day and single day hiking trails**, the majority of them providing access to beaches offering absolute solitude. **Abel Tasman Coast Track** will take three to five days with many beach crossing dependent on the tide. A real adventure in unspoiled nature.

Chapter 8
South of Christchurch Including Queenstown and Around

The West Coast National Parks near Queenstown

Flying into Queenstown offers a remarkable vista, the white tinged peaks and exposed fjordlands dazzling beneath the wingtips. Queenstown and the far south is New Zealand at its most naturally primitive and dramatic, the landscapes virtually uninhabited as they cascade into the South Pacific. This is a land untamed; rugged peaks, white wonderlands, mountain passes that become impassable for half the year. Unsurprisingly, this is also New Zealand's adventure capital. Queenstown self-proclaims itself the adrenalin capital of the world, and anyone who visits is unlikely to argue. Spectacular hiking trails cross the mountains, jet boats skid across lakes, and the world's first ever commercial bungee jump can be found here. This is also where you'll discover the country's ski slopes and best winter snow season.

Yet for all the adventure, this chapter continues New Zealand's trend of tranquility. Alpine lakes reflect the mountain summits and the solitude is practically absolute. As an example, Queenstown is the major town here and it's little more than four blocks square. Many people become immediately hypnotized by this region and find it difficult to leave. Days roll into weeks as the adrenalin finds an antidote with the ubiquitous serenity.

This chapter covers everything in New Zealand south of Christchurch. All these destinations can be accessed as (often long) day trips from Queenstown. These destinations can also be explored in a loop using State Highways 1, 8 and 6, from Queenstown. The most popular one way route is to travel north from Queenstown on SH6 through two of the West Coast parks; or use SH8 to visit Mount Cook and then cross to Christchurch. The chapter is sub-divided into three distinct areas. Queenstown and around provides the entry point and base. Three dramatic yet often inaccessible national parks line the West Coast, then a series of winding national roads connect the eastern half of this remote region.

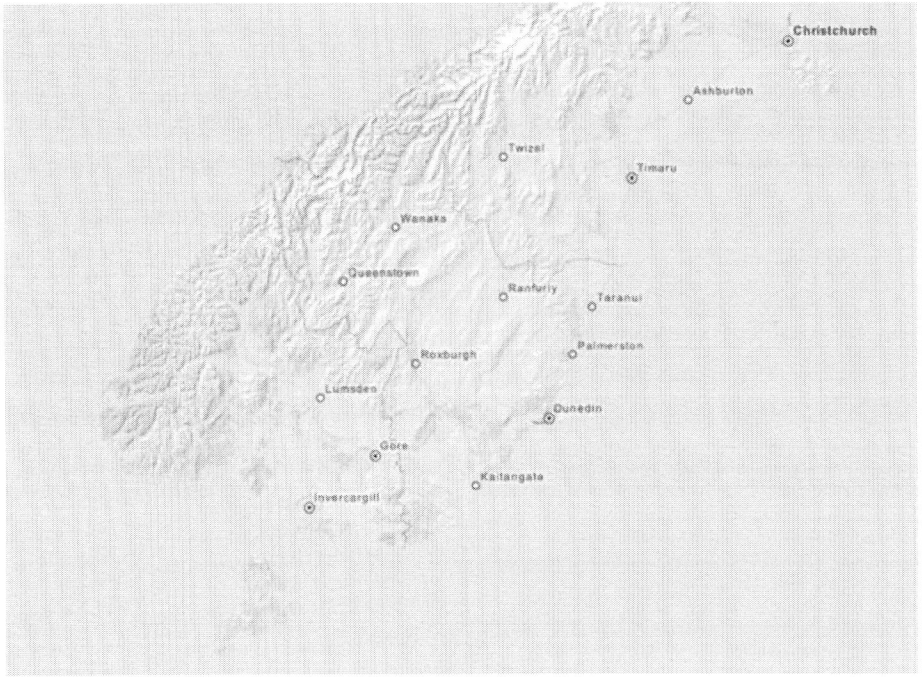

©openstreetmap contributors

Travel Essentials for South of Christchurch Including Queenstown and Around

Getting Here: Queenstown International Airport has direct connections to Australia and the rest of New Zealand. Coming by road there's little chance of getting lost, as there's only a couple of routes through the mountains.

Getting Around: Roads are few and far between, usually winding long paths around the mountains and meaning the journey often takes double the time you expect them to. Public transport is at its most infrequent and it's difficult to get anywhere fast. However, the roads in this part of New Zealand are amongst the most scenic in the world. In particular, any journey into the Fjordlands or along SH6 is a delight, traversing mesmerizing mountain scenery and connecting endless expanses of national park.

Planning an Itinerary: The Queenstown base is good for organizing tours to almost everywhere within the region, including guided hiking and the all the adrenalin activities. However, these can often be long full day tours with the travel involved. More than any other region, this area is best suited to renting your own vehicle. With your own wheels the exploration is endless, however, public transport struggles to connect everywhere and tours can become pricey.

Accommodation South of Christchurch Including Queenstown and Around: A real mixed bag here. You can find the full range in Queenstown, from boutique 5* hotels to cheap party hostels on the lake. Head into the national parks and accommodation is scarce, with mountain huts for self-sufficient hikers the most likely place to lay your head.

South of Christchurch Including Queenstown and Around

Tucked between the mountains and framed by a dazzling alpine lake, Queenstown is perhaps New Zealand's most synonymous destination. Self proclaimed the adrenalin capital of the world, and the home of commercial bungee jumping, it's also a wonderfully idyllic and quiet destination. It is a tourist centered town and the number of tour companies and activities on offer can make the credit card weep. You'll have no problem organizing your activities. The challenge is often choosing between half a dozen companies offering a slant on the same thing. Having said that, the town doesn't feel swamped or overly commercialized. The location alone is enough to inspire every visitor and the surrounding area ensures that most stay for more than a few days. Note that Queenstown is cold in winter, dropping below freezing on most nights.

The Remarkables Mountain Range above Lake Wakatipu.

- You may have recognized the scenery around Queenstown. The **Remarkables Mountain Range** that towers above Lake Wakatipu has features in dozens of movies and adverts. This dazzling setting is enough to charm any visitor and it's best viewed by either wandering the **lakeshore path** out of Queenstown or taking the **Skyline Gondola** up the mountain. Arrive at the summit and for $15 you can indulge in a bit of **luge racing** – it sounds dramatic but is for the whole family. There's an expensive cafe up here but it's worth it for the views.

- Queenstown offers New Zealand's premier **skiing** with the season officially running from mid-June to early October. However, July and August are the most solid bets given inconsistent recent winters. Queenstown's streets are filled with ski and snowboard operators who rent out equipment, provide transport to the lifts, and offer **heli skiing** trips to the experienced. **Coronet Peak and Cardrona** are in season for longest. **Lake Wanaka** and **Remarkables** receive constantly good reports for powder and range of slopes.

- The nearby forests are where orcas fought hobbits in the Lord of the Rings and **movie location tours** also reveal a plethora of places from Peter Jackson's and other directors' movies. Most visitors are surprised at how much is filmed in this part of New Zealand.

- **Tandem parasailing** from this mountain is increasingly popular and offers dazzling birds-eye views of lake and mountains. There's fierce competition between half a dozen companies that offer the same flights. Companies also offer tandem hang gliding flights.

- Queenstown was where the world's first commercial bungee jump took place and is the first home of A.J Hackett's bungee operation. There are three **bungee jumps** to choose from; the original on **Kawarau Bridge**, a newer 134meter jump from a suspended cable car, and a shorter jump above Queenstown from besides the gondola station. In addition, they now operate two bungee swings, including New Zealand's highest. Transport to the jumps is included but note that it can be a 4 -5 hour trip in total. For something quicker, take the jump and swing from the gondola station above town. A.J Hackett isn't the only bungee jumping company in town. There's also the Shotover Canyon Swing

- Jet boating is another unique Queenstown invention. Essentially, a 16 person speed boat skids along alpine rivers, pulling hand break turns and veering through canyons to the scared delight of passengers. **Shotover River Jet** is the oldest and was even visited by Queen Elizabeth II. However, there are cheaper and longer rides that head out on Lake Wakatipu or onto **Skippers Canyon**. Note that you hand over all control to the skipper and this is the one New Zealand activity without a 100% safety record.

- Queenstown's adrenalin paradigm is infectious and most people end up far from their comfort zone, carried away on the wave of buzzed up tourists filling the bars and hotels. So don't be too surprised when you end up on a **tandem skydive** from 15,000ft.

- An excellent collection of **fine dining restaurants** can be found along the small harbor, the pubs are renowned for **5am weekend parties**, and if you see a queue on the street it's probably for **Fergburger**, a nationwide institution and perhaps the finest burgers to be found in the Southern Hemisphere.

- A large handful of **micro flight** and **helicopter** companies have their base in Queenstown. Some focus on set routes into the Fjordlands (see below) while others design custom itineraries across the whole of the far south. It's the most spectacular means of experiencing the whole of the south but it comes with a hefty price tag. See the sections below for the kind of landscapes these flights traverse. Note that the weather isn't always conducive to aerial experiences so it pays to be flexible with your itinerary.

- Despite the thrills and spills, Queenstown is a small and relaxed town, the reflections in Lake Wakatipu enough to sooth any over the top stimulation. Many people use Queenstown as a **base to explore the whole region with day trips and tours**. This is particularly true for those on public transport.

- Just north of Queenstown is historic **Arrowtown**, a cute place for a cafe lunch or winery visit. Hire a mountain bike here and you're deep in the Middle Earth scenery within moments.

Recognize this? This was the setting of the swamps in Peter Jackson's Lord of the Rings. Just outside Queenstown.

- This Central Otago region is home to the **world's southernmost wine region**. A mosaic of unusual soils and conditions make this a place for experimentation and unique wines. Wine connoisseurs find it difficult not to sample the inimitability on offer, although this doesn't have the same wine appeal to newcomers as Hawkes Bay or Marlborough. There are a range of wineries running between Queenstown, Arrowtown, and Cromwell.

The West Coast National Parks

The Southwestern coastline offers some of the world's most dramatic landscapes, marked by fjords, precipitous mountains, subtropical rainforest, and glaciers. Together, they form one of the world's largest national park areas, with the Fjordland National Park alone covering over 1.2 million hectares. The majority of this area is unexplored and uninhabited and it's difficult to imagine a more pristine or complete impression of wilderness. Unsurprising, this whole section of New Zealand is a UNESCO World Heritage Site.

A total of four national parks share boundaries along the Southwestern coast. This section has been sub-divided to provide individual information about each of them. Their remoteness is central to their primitive beauty, however, it poses challenges for independent exploration. These parks are presented from south to north.

Traveling Between the National Parks: These parks are divided by huge mountain chains and there is no obvious route that connects all four, other than multi-day hiking trails. Fjordland National Park has no road access north so you must return to Queenstown and SH6 or SH8. Choosing one of these two roads will undoubtedly define your route. SH6 weaves alongside and through Mount Aspiring National Park, before hugging the coastline and reaching Westland Tai Poutini National Park. With this route it's a long way north and then back south to add Christchurch into the itinerary. Alternatively, SH8 offers an easy connection to Mount Cook National Park and the Christchurch.

Fjordland National Park

Despite the 500kms of walking tracks and popularity of Milford Sound, the Fjordlands are vastly unexplored and unchartered. It's an almost mythical expanse of narrow fjords, shining glaciers, and stark mountains that rise vertically and keep rising. Few world landscapes can compare and it's a premier highlight of the whole country, despite the 8 meters of annual rainfall that dumps on the land during 200 rainy days.

Access to Fjordland National Park: Te Anau is the park's gateway and lies on State Highway 94. It's easy to reach from Queenstown. The challenge is how to go further, and you'll probably need an organized tour to see more, other than self driving the mountain passes to Milford Sound.

- A number of companies offer **scenic flights** through the Fjordlands (see also Queenstown). While they cost upwards of $600 it can be worth the price. Touch down on isolated glaciers, swoop low through the fjords, and get an overarching impression of the Fjordland's scale. The inclement

81

weather can sometimes dampen the experience. A good option is to head out to the Fjordlands by road and then organize a flight back to Queenstown if the weather is looking good.

- **Milford Sound** was New Zealand's entry in the new seven wonders of the world contest. With the mist veiling a narrow canyon, this fjord (it was erroneously called a sound by the first Europeans to see it) is the narrowest and most dramatic of the whole national park. **Boat cruises** take 60 – 90 minutes to tour the fjord, including seal colonies, 400 meter waterfalls, and where the fjord waters meet the Tasman Sea. All-inclusive tours leave daily from Queenstown and take around 12 hours, including a few stops on route out and the boat trip. A more immersive experience is the overnight boat cruises which allow you to wake up shrouded in Milford's famous mist.

A boat cruise on Milford Sound.

- **Te Puau** is a quiet base for Fjordland exploration, situated on Lake Te Anau. Even smaller is **Manapouri**, another unblemished spot with lake views. Both are particularly impressive for those on public transport wanting an authentic immersion in the Fjordlands scenery.

- Cruise the waters of **Doubtful Sound**, the region's second fjord that was mistakenly called a sound. Doubtful isn't as dramatic as Milford, however, the boats are smaller and it feels more like an off the beaten track adventure. You first cross **Lake Manapuri** and stop at the hydro-electric power station, then cross **Wilmott Pass** to Doubtful Sound where the journey passes dolphin pods on route to the Tasman Sea. Like Milford, an overnight cruise really imbues the feeling of getting lost in wild landscapes.

- The Fjordlands become a hiker's mecca during summer and a number of tracks traverse the triangular peaks, each with dazzling views onto the fjords. Most famous is the **Milford Track**, a four day hike with accommodation at mountain huts on route. It constantly holds its place in the top echelons of world hiking routes. The **Routeburn Track** joins the Fjordlands with Mount Aspiring National Park, and the **Hollyford** and **Hump Ridge Track** also offer multi-day hiking in the Fjordlands. All accommodation must be pre-booked. These are challenging hikes and those without experience are recommended to take a guide.

Mount Aspiring National Park

Mount Aspiring provides a halfway between the glaciers and white wonderland of the Fjordlands and the gouged valleys of Mount Cook. Like the Fjordlands it's remote and difficult to tame, a haven for intrepid hikers and those with a few days to put aside to adventure. While Mount Aspiring doesn't have the fjords, it still features vast snowfields, glaciers, and an inspiring mountain range.

Access to Mount Aspiring National Park: Unfortunately it's not as easy as continuing north from Milford Sound and the Fjordlands. The only direct route between the two parks is the three day Routeburn walking track. Mount Aspiring is easy to reach from Queenstown. Either journey along Lake Wakatipu to Paradise (yes, that's a real place) and then the small settlement of Glenorchy. Most feasible and more popular is using Wanaka as your base, it's on the SH6 and the journey can continue from here to Westland Tai Poutini National Park.

- Mount Aspiring is a real **hiker's wonderland** with a range of multi-day treks utilizing mountain huts. The **Rees-Dart track** is perhaps the most spectacular. From a base in Wanaka three good half day hikes give a glimpse of this wilderness; **Beacon Point Walk**, **Aspiring Hut walk** and the

Rob Roy track. Note that most trails are only open during summer from November to March.

- **Wanaka** itself is a delightful town on the lakeside, surrounded by white-tinged mountains and a good alternative for those who think Queenstown has too many tourists. **Glenorchy** is a more exclusive base with a lack of low to mid range accommodation.

- Get very wet and abseil, slide, jump, and dive through **Deep Canyon** near Wanaka. This **canyoning** experience is up there on the South Island Adrenalin meter.

- Like Queenstown, Wanaka has its fair share of s**kydiving, scenic flights, boat cruises, kayaking, and four wheeled adventure tours**. They're all less popular and this might suit some visitors – it feels more like wilderness when there isn't 20 other people in your tour group. Everything is easy to organize in the town and it's good to check out everything on offer before handing over the credit card. Each year a new operator brings out a new adventure to try in Mount Aspiring.

- The **jet boating in Mount Aspiring** is more remote than what's on offer in Queenstown. Half and full day trips combine hiking and scenic drives, making a good way to experience Mount Aspiring without committing too much time or money.

- Exceptional **heli skiing** can be done on the **Northern Buchanans** and **Albertburn**, remote areas in the national park. It can be organized in Queenstown and Wanaka.

Westland Tai Poutini National Park

The high Southern Alps and peaks of Mount Cook spill down into the Tasman Sea, forming a primeval landscape of glaciers, sub-tropical rainforest, lakes, and then beaches engulfed by roaring wind. For scenic diversity it's unbeatable, with the SH6 highway ensuring you don't need private transport to journey through the treasure trove of visual highlights. Two accessible glaciers then provide the main attractions.

Access to Westland Tai Poutini National Park: Coming from Mount Aspiring National Park, the SH6 hits the coastline and heads straight through the national park. It's also easy to head south from Greymouth (see chapter 7) on the SH6, 60 miles north of the park. However, if you're not already on the West Coast then accessing this park can be time consuming as it's a long roundabout route to reach the SH6.

- The **journey to Westland Tai Poutini National Park on SH6** is one of New Zealand's finest. Coming from the south you're permanently engulfed in the mountain wonderland. Arrive from Greyton in the north (see chapter 7) and it's equally spectacular, domineering summits and then turquoise lakes as you enter the park.

- Two dazzling glaciers form the park's centerpieces, **Franz Josef Glacier** and **Fox Glacier**. Both are among the most accessible glaciers to visit in the world and over 1000 visitors a day hike on the exposed ice. Both have their own village with a range of accommodation, tour companies, and a couple of restaurants. Visitors usually pick one as they offer similar experiences:

  o **Franz Josef** is more spectacular due to its steeper walls. It's also more unstable and a short helicopter ride takes visitors over the steep terminal face for a two hour hike between the icefalls, including walking through ice tunnels. You'll need ice axes and crampons for the dramatic journey. This is the more expensive of the glaciers to visit.

  o **Fox Glacier** is even more accessible and it's possible to walk unguided from the village to the glacier face. However, a guide is always recommended and unguided tourists have died here, crushed beneath ice fall after crossing safety barriers. Without a guide, it's absolutely essential to stay within the clearly marked areas. Hiring crampons is also recommended. Fox Glacier tumbles onto the rainforest, making an iconic sight. However, the ease of access sometimes makes it difficult to get a photo without other tourists.

- Both villages offer a sublime array of **hiking trails**, the majority of them short and more suited to novice hikers than the other national parks. Almost all of them provide vistas onto rainforest, sapphire lakes with perfect reflections, and views onto the glacier. For views all the way from mountain to sea try **Okarito Trig, Mount Fox**, or **Alex Knob. Lake Mathe-**

son is another achievable and beautiful day hike. Visitor's centers and accommodation in both of the villages provide detailed information and maps.

- Near to Fox Glacier is **Gillespies Beach**, a rocky opening fringed by even wilder coast and clean crisp waters. Not for sunbathing, but turn around and take in the views of the peaks and park.

Aoroki / Mount Cook National Park and the Mackenzie District

Rising 3,724meters, New Zealand's highest peak towers above the Southern Alps and the surrounding fertile valleys. Mount Cook is just one of 19 high summits and any interlude from mountain is provided by gaping glacier. This park is smaller than its neighbors, the focus very much on permanently white summits, hiking, and two turquoise blue lakes in its vicinity. It's also the most accessible and easy to explore for families and those on public transport.

Access to Aoroki / Mount Cook National Park: Perhaps the park's greatest appeal is its accessibility. There are few other places in the world where such a conglomeration of peaks and glaciers can be found within two to three hours of the city (Christchurch or Queenstown). The road is winding and quiet from either base. However, taking this inland route to Mount Cook means it's difficult to reach Mount Aspiring or Westland Tai Poutini without a long detour.

- **Mount Cook** is the obvious aesthetic highlight, although unless you're on a **scenic flight** (arranged at Mount Cook Village or Twizel) or a skilled mountaineer, you'll be viewing it from below. The national park contains **19 different 3000 meter plus peaks** and the country's largest glaciers. From almost any angle it feels like you're in a white wonderland, even in mid-summer.

- The Department of Conservation park base is an excellent source of information and starting point for adventures in the park. Ten different **day walks** head out from here, with a number of them being suitable for families. In addition, there are countless **mountain bikes trails**. Experienced hikers can take one of three **multi-day alpine hiking trails** with accommodation on route in the park huts.

- **Mount Cook Village** is purely for the benefit of tourists but it forms a cute enough base and the only village in the national park. Prices are higher than elsewhere but there is a range of accommodation from hostels to 5* options. It's easy to organize all activities from here. **Twizel** is the closest base outside the park and its setting is almost as charming. Accommodation is cheaper here and a full range of tour operators can be found.

- Gaze across the turquoise waters of **Lake Tekapo** and you're unlikely to move for a few days. New Zealand's highest large lake is serenity personified and **Tekapo** village maintains the equanimity. Many **boat activities** can be organized here and it's a good base for Mount Cook if you have your own transport.

- **Star gazing** is a preserved past time around here with artificial lighting deliberately minimized and all streetlights being down facing. Every clear evening brings a starry wonderland overhead. To ascertain what you're looking at, visit the **Hermitage Hotel's planetarium** and use the telescopes.

The Far South

Rarely visited and well off the tourist trail, the southeast of the South Island doesn't share the same wondrous landscapes of the West Coast. It's undeniably pleasant and equally secluded, however, most visitors choose to skip through the East on route to the national parks of the West. The attractions lie in journeying through rugged landscapes and soaking up the quaint atmosphere on route. It feels like a journey back in time, probably 200 years back in time given the rurality and iconicity.

Destinations in this section are presented south to north. The advantage of the East Coast are the easier road connections to Christchurch and the north. All the destinations are located on, or within easy reach of, SH1. Perhaps the most popular loop on the South Island is to journey south from Christchurch on SH1, then use SH6 to connect with Queenstown and the West Coast National Parks before returning to Christchurch. The loop works equally well from Queenstown.

- The country's third largest island, **Stewart Island** lies one hour boat ride south of Invercargill. Windswept, jagged, cold; this is real immersion in the sub-antarctic and usually only visited by outdoor enthusiasts seeking pure escapism. There's a remarkable beauty here but you must come prepared. Even more challenging are the uninhabited **Sub-Antarctic Islands** lying further south; access by permit only, obtainable in Invercargill or Stewart Island.

- **Invarcargill** is a small town on the far southern tip of the South Island. There's little to see but it marks the start (or end dependent on your perspective) of both SH1 and SH6 roads. From here it's about 10 miles out to **Bluff**, the very edge of the island and views across stunning windswept coastline.

- SH1 takes a relatively direct route to Dunedin, but for absolute solitude and New Zealand's forgotten coastline, those with transport can take the three hour detour via **Catlins Conservation Park**.

- Frolicking in its colonial history and bursting with party happy students, **Dunedin** is the main town in this region. Easy walks take you along the **Otago Peninsula,** or to **Tunnel Beach**, a place for admiring the coastline rather than catching rays. **Olveston** and the **Toitu Otago Settlers Museum** provide a fascinating narrative on the town's history. The former showcases old-world opulence, the latter offers a more socially rounded story. In a vastly uninhabited region, Dunedin is also the place to hit the **pubs** and enjoy **international cuisine**.

- **Oamaru** takes prizes for quirkiness and always brings a smile to anyone who stops. Its **Victorian Precinct** really does feel Victorian and a living relic from the 19th century, then its juxtaposed with **Steampunk HQ**, a larger than life art gallery that's ever so slightly warped. There's a train that blows fire and a concoction of punk art with humorous tones. Just out of town, and easy to visit by taxi, bus, or a long hike, you'll find the mischievous **blue penguin colony** and the surreal **Moeraki Boulders**.

- Just south of Oamaru, SH1 meets **SH85**, a picturesque (aren't they all?) **route west to Alexandra and then Queenstown**. There are mountain bike trails and tiny farm settlements, and not much else before you hit the vineyards and old towns near Queenstown.

- From Oamaru most people head direct to Christchurch, the potential stop on route being **Timaru**, a village with sweeping ocean views.

Conclusion
Aren't You Excited? Your Trip Is About to Begin!

Well, you've made it. You've read through New Zealand, north to south, and hopefully you're reading this with a soporific lake mountain vista in the background. Thanks for reading. Seriously. If you weren't reading then we wouldn't be writing and continuing our theme of off the beaten track guides aimed at anyone with an adventurous spirit. Hopefully your current backdrop is a New Zealand one, whether that's the wild West Coast national parks, a fertile row of vines, or somewhere volcanic in the north. If your current backdrop isn't in New Zealand then fear not, your time will come, and hopefully this guidebook will be all your need to explore this country of wonder.

We're always keen to gather your feedback. Like we've said, we're only writing because so many of you are reading. And what's the point writing a guidebook if there isn't a desire to always improve and inspire. The purpose of this guidebook is to provide all the information you need to get out and explore New Zealand, with the excellent visitor information centers providing extremely detailed and free localized information to complement this guide. We hope it worked for you. If it didn't, then please let us know.

That's it from us. Thank you again for reading and if you liked it, check out the rest of our travel guides as you continue the intrepid exploration of our planet.

Learn Any Language 300% FASTER

>> Get Full Online Language Courses With Audio Lessons <<

Would you like to learn a new language before you start your trip? I think that's a great idea. Now, why don't you do it 300% *FASTER*?

I've partnered with the most revolutionary language teachers to bring you the very language online courses I've ever seen. It's a mind-blowing program specifically created for language hackers such as ourselves. It will allow you learn ANY language, from French to Chinese, 3x faster, straight from the comfort of your own home, office, or wherever you may be. It's like having an unfair advantage!

You can choose from a wide variety of languages, such as French, Spanish, Italian, German, Chinese, Portuguese, and A TON more.

Each Online Course consists of:

+ 91 Built-In Lessons
+ 33 Interactive Audio Lessons
+ 24/7 Support to Keep You Going

The program is extremely engaging, fun, and easy-going. You won't even notice you are learning a complex foreign language from scratch. And before you realize it, by the time you go through all the lessons you will officially become a truly solid speaker.

Old classrooms are a thing of the past. It's time for a revolution.

If you'd like to go the extra mile, then follow the link below, and let the revolution begin!

>> http://www.bitly.com/foreign-language-courses <<

CHECK OUT THE COURSE »

Ps: Can I Ask You A Quick Favor?

If you liked the book, please leave a nice review on Amazon! I'd absolutely love to hear your feedback. Every time I read your reviews... you make me smile. I'd be immensely thankful if you go to Amazon now, and write down a quick line sharing with me your experience. I personally read ALL the reviews there, and I'm thrilled to hear your feedback and honest motivation. It's what keeps me going, and helps me improve everyday =)

Please go Amazon now and drop a quick review sharing your experience!

***

THANKS!

***

ONCE YOU'RE BACK,
FLIP THE PAGE!
BONUS CHAPTER AHEAD
=)

Preview Of "Thailand For Tourists - The Traveler's Travel Guide to Make the Most Out of Your Trip to Thailand - Where to Go, Eat, Sleep & Party"

Introduction
Why You Will Fall in Love with Thailand

Welcome to Thailand!

Thailand has become famous as a prime backpacker getaway with tropical climate, stunning views, and cheap wild parties that make it the ultimate destination in Southeast Asia. It tops the charts with beautiful beaches and a vibrant nightlife that welcomes tourists looking for a good time. Catering to travelers on shoestring budgets as well as those seeking a luxurious holiday, Thailand has something for everyone with picture-perfect beauty, exotic tastes and cultural sights around every corner. No matter what kind of traveler or tourist you are Thailand has something for you.

For the past few decades Thailand has been politically stable with a booming economy and the influx of tourists searching for the next Full Moon Party have made it the top destination in Southeast Asia. The year-round tropical weather makes it a sunny, warm escape that has many people extending their stays and coming back for more. With 1,430 islands in Thailand there are plenty of sandy beaches to accommodate the 26+ million tourists visiting every year, and in 2013 it was the tenth most visited country in the world.

This guide provides an overview of the different regions of Thailand including how to get there, what to see and do, and when to go. If you're looking for logistical information about the country and its customs check out the chapter titled Tips and Tricks. So dive right in and plan your ultimate adventure to Thailand, and prepare to be amazed.

Regions

Thailand is divided into six geographic regions, Northern, Central, Eastern, Issan, and Southern. North Thailand is situated in the mountains and is known for trekking, outdoor adventures and cultural excursions to experience life in the hill tribes. Within the north is the historically infamous Golden Triangle, once known for its opium production and now a popular tourist destination. To learn more about what North Thailand has to offer, check out the chapter on North Thailand.

Central Thailand is home to Bangkok, the capital, a common starting point for many visitors. It boasts an active nightlife with many museums and historical sights. East Thailand is a small region to the southeast of Bangkok and boasts numerous beaches and coastline. Issan is in the far east, bordering Cambodia, and its Khmer ruins and agriculture are often overlooked by travelers. The chapter in this guide on Central Thailand combines three of these three regions, Central, East and Issan.

South Thailand is famous for its beaches, islands and the Full Moon Parties that draw many visitors every year. There is an abundance of snorkeling, scuba diving, and even some surfing with small waves which make it a great place to learn.

The weather and the rainy season in Thailand vary by region and by time of year so check the weather before you plan your trip. Since Northern Thailand is mountainous it is generally cooler than the rest of the country, while the southern coasts and islands are warmer all year round. The weather can be different on the islands too which are subject to occasional tsunamis.

Getting between the different regions can be an adventure in itself. There are many low-cost airlines that will fly you from Chiang Mai to Bangkok and on to Phuket, and many other destinations. You can also choose to take the train which, while it may take more time than a bus, is generally safer than driving on the Thai roads. It is most common to travel by road and there are a myriad of options to get around, from buses with VIP seats to minivans and three-wheeled tuk-tuks that look like a motorcycle pulling a small carriage. There are ferries connecting the islands to the mainland that run regularly, though more frequently during the high season. At your destination you can easily get around with taxis, buses, tuk-tuks and on foot. It is also popular to rent a car or a motorcycle for traveling on your own schedule but be sure to take proper care if you are considering this route. See Tips and Tricks for more information.

A Brief History

Located just north of the equator Thailand is bordered by Myanmar (Burma) to the northwest, Laos to the northeast, Cambodia to the east, and Malaysia to the south. It lies between the Gulf of Thailand in the east and the Andaman Sea in the west. A little bigger in size than Spain, Thailand's population has nearly doubled since 1970 to approximately 67 million. Nearly three quarters of the population are ethnic Thai with the remaining population a mix of Chinese, Thai-Chinese, Malay and smaller groups of other expats. More than 95% are Theravada Buddhist, one of two major branches within Buddhism, which has heavily influenced the culture. Thai cuisine reflects the cultural influences from countries like Malaysia, Cambodia, Myanmar and China, making Thai food a culinary mix of spicy, sweet, sour, and bitter flavors.

The word "thai" means free and therefore "Thailand" means land of the free which is an appropriate name as it is the only country in Southeast Asia that has never been occupied by foreign powers, a point of pride with the Thai people. You will quickly notice that the people are very outwardly upbeat and smiley, hardworking and pleasant overall. Thai people say "mai pen rai" which means "ok", "nevermind" or "it's not a problem" but more than that it encompasses the focus of their lives that they are to be enjoyed and not filled with worries.

Prior to 1949 Thailand was known as Siam to the rest of the world. The term Siamese twins comes from two famous Thai brothers, Chang and Eng, who were attached at the midsection and traveled in a circus in the 1800's. Currently Thailand is ruled by King Bhumibol Adulyadej of the Chakri dynasty who took the throne in 1946. He is the longest-serving head of state that is currently in office and, although it is a constitutional monarchy, it is against the law to criticize the monarchy.

During World War 2 Thailand allied with Japan and after the war became an ally of the United States. Since the 1980s it has undergone extensive modernization and development which boosted the economy and Thailands' global presence. In the last six years there has been growing anti-government sentiment and in the spring of 2014 there was a military coup d'état. There were protests and other unrest but since then Thailand has restabilized and the events did not generally affect tourists.

As a backpacker mecca there are many low budget travelers from all over the world. Chinese nationals make up the largest percentage of visitors, followed by (in order) Malaysia, Russia, Japan, South Korea, Laos, India, Australia, Singapore, United Kingdom, USA, Vietnam, Germany and France.

Thailand is certainly still an inexpensive getaway but depending on your activities and the time of the year you can still manage to spend a medium chunk of change on your vacation. However with a little careful planning you can travel comfortably on a moderate budget or even a shoestring. This guide is for all types of travelers whether you are a strapped for cash backpacker who spent most of your money on the flight or you've saved for this trip and you're ready to let loose. You'll be hitting the big parties and in Thailand the sky's the limit.

In short, Thailand is a country for everyone. With such a variety of places, attractions, landscapes and cultures to experience you may need to plan a few trips to Thailand. Don't despair, keep reading and you will find all the information you need on how to make the most out of your trip to Thailand, a trip you will never forget (or won't remember).

Chapter 1
How to Make the Most Out of This Guide

This guide contains a broad range of information to aid you as your plan your trip to Thailand. Each section has valuable information on how to make the most out of your holiday with insider tips and background information on Thailand all in one digestible guide. There are so many destinations in Thailand that it can be difficult to decide which ones are right for you. This guide will help you narrow down what you want to see and do while providing insight into how to have the ultimate trip.

Since Thailand has been such a popular destination for the last few decades there is a wealth of information out there in the form of formal guidebooks, personal travel blogs, and official Thai websites. There are hotels and hostels dotting the tourist trail and plenty of transportation options to take you from the mountains to the cities to the islands. Thailand remains a low cost destination that attracts all sorts of travelers, from backpackers to divers to business travelers to families, and this guide was written with all of them in mind. Whether you like to book everything in advance or land and figure things out as you go this guide will help you find your way.

To help you start the planning process, Chapter 3 gives an overview of things to know and how to get started with your planning your trip. There is information about entrance requirements, what to pack, what NOT to pack, and other useful tidbits on where to go in the amount of time you have.

Chapter 4 covers the north of Thailand and gives a rundown of the most common sights and activities in the hills. There are treks, motorbikes, rafting, and even cooking classes all waiting for you to explore! Thailand borders with Laos and Myanmar in the north so while most tourists come from Bangkok there are also many connections to the neighboring countries.

Nearly all visitors pass through the capital at least once so to learn about the sights, sounds, smells and sensations of Bangkok check out Chapter 5. There are many great day trips out of Bangkok so if you have a few extra days then consider visiting the floating markets of Damnoen Saduak and Amphawa, and the old capital of Thailand at Ayutthaya.

The highlight of Thailand for many is Chapter 6, the islands, beaches and southern coast. You can skip ahead to this chapter if that is what you have been waiting for but don't forget to skim through the rest, Thailand is a diverse area with a lot more than just great scuba diving (though it has that too).

Chapter 7 covers some of the logistical and cultural information about Thailand. Though Thailand is a relatively safe country the laws and customs are different than in the western world so read through in order to be prepared. There are also many scams that have been cleverly devised for parting holidaymakers from their cash and you can read an overview of the most common ones there.

There are a few more controversial topics in Thailand that are addressed in Chapter 8. Thailand has occasionally become synonymous with prostitution and drug use, neither of which are actually legal but both happen frequently. There are also many cultural and animal attractions for visitors that you should consider carefully before taking part.

Chapter 9 is a bonus section that covers the most useful Thai words and phrases that will help you ease your way around the country. The pronunciation can be quite difficult so the guide simplifies it considerably so that you can pick up a few words before you go. Once you arrive you can practice and learn even more from the native speakers themselves.

Chapter 2
Let's Start At the Beginning - Planning Your Trip

Thailand is fairly easy to visit, most nationalities can enter without a visa and stay for up to a month. You will need a return flight or proof of onward travel from Thailand to assure authorities that you intend to leave. Your passport must be valid for 6 months from the date of entry and you need one free visa page for the entry stamp.

There are no recommended vaccinations or medications that you will need to take besides some calcium for any upset stomachs and a little aspirin for those hangovers. Pharmacies are easy to find in big cities should you run out of painkillers from too many drinks the previous night.

When planning your destinations and activities think about what things or places you absolutely want to see and do, then build the rest of the trip around that. If you are crunched for time then you may want to consider taking some domestic flights to get between locations. If you have more flexibility then you can take more side trips and travel slower. On a whim you can extend your stay and go for the advanced diving course if the open-water scuba certification went well.

Here are some example itineraries to give you an idea of what you can see and do in different periods of time. Remember that you could face jet lag when flying from North America or Europe so give yourself a day or two to recover so you can hit the road running later.

Two weeks on the islands

Once you fly into Bangkok don't rush away just yet, spend some time exploring the city and all the sights it has to offer. Bangkok has earned its reputation as the "city of sin" in Asia so drop by Patong to get an idea how it got that nickname. After you have had your fill you can take an overnight bus down to the coasts to go diving in Koh Tao or to the infamous Ko Pha Ngan for some full mooning. When you've had your fill of parties and snorkeling then cross over to the Andaman coast to see the limestone cliffs and the quieter beaches. You can go rock climbing in Rai leh with the pros or find a peaceful bit of coast on Ko Lanta. You will find plenty to keep you occupied for two weeks or more without difficulty.

Two weeks North and South

For those looking to see a broader spectrum of Thailand with friendly people and great food then consider getting a taste of Thailand from north to south. Bangkok is a busy city with a lot to see like Wat Pho and the Grand Palace, exciting neighborhoods and plenty of shopping. If malls aren't your cup of tea then you can get out of Bangkok sooner and head for hills after just a few days. You can take a bus, train or plane up to Chiang Mai either in a matter of hours or overnight. There are many activities in and around Chiang Mai and numerous nearby destinations like Pai, the backpacker hangout, and motorbiking around Mae Hong Son. You can easily spend anywhere from a few days to two weeks in the north and always find new things to discover.

The final ingredient of an unforgettable trip to Thailand are the islands. There are many to choose from like the touristy Phuket, the popular Koh Samui and the wild Ko Pha Ngan. If you are short on time then the best plan is to find the right island for you and camp out there. For those with more time then you can venture out into the island hopping experience.

One month to see it all

For those who mean serious business when it comes to vacation you are lucky to be able to spend it in such a wonderful country. Like the others start with a few days in Bangkok and take your time traveling north, there are many great side trips along the way. Once you hit Chiang Mai you can find some great trekking and the multi-day excursions are a great way to see the views.

When you're ready to sunbathe head to the coasts. You can visit Koh Samui to party, Koh Pha Ngan to party harder and Ko Tao to get away from it all under the sea. On the west coast you can go to Ko Phi Phi, one of the prettiest spots in all of Thailand. If you have some baht to burn you can stay at ocean view resorts and listen to the waves as you fall asleep. You have plenty of time to take the slow road while you travel between destinations and that can be a worthwhile adventure on its own.

Regardless of how long your trip is remember that less is more. Pack less than you think you will need, you can always buy it there. Don't try to see too many things in one day as you won't enjoy them as much. Plan regular rest days so that you can put your feet up and catch up on sleep. Also account for travel time, you don't want to be traveling for 12 hours every other day so make sure you have at least a few days between long travel days or nights.

Transportation

You have many options for getting around Thailand and all of the tourist destinations are well connected. You can fly from the north and the south to Bangkok on one of the many low-cost carriers like Bangkok Airways, Thai Airways, Thai Smile and many more. There are buses running from Bangkok to most cities in the north and south with many comfortable overnight buses for the long hauls. You can book your tickets a few days in advance if you have a specific schedule but if you have more flexibility then you can usually go to the station the day before or the day of and find plenty of options, particularly between the popular routes of Bangkok to Chiang Mai and Bangkok toward the islands.

If trains are more your style then Thailand is a great place to hit the rails for very cheap. Trains have three classes of cars: 1st with air conditioned sleepers for overnight trains, 2nd class has seat and sleeper options some with air conditioning, and 3rd class which is perfectly fine for shorter trips. Most foreigners find that the 2nd class sleepers are perfectly comfortable and a great way to experience authentic Thai travel. Backpackers on a tighter budget should consider the 3rd class, it is a very clean and easy way to get around. You can book your tickets at the train station though if you are traveling during the holidays then you may want to book farther in advance.

Costs

Thailand is not an expensive country and you can have quite a comfortable trip for a lot less than in other parts of the world. Depending on your budget you can find accommodation for as little as $4 a night or as much as a few thousand dollars. Generally speaking a comfortable budget is about $50 per day per person. This includes some internal flights to save time on transportation and some tours and activities, whether it is multi-day hiking trips or scuba diving in the south. With that budget you can eat some street food but also dine on some of the nicer offerings in Bangkok and the other cities. You can stay at comfortable guesthouses and even splurge for a beach bungalow here and there.

If you are on a tighter budget you can certainly travel and enjoy Thailand for less money per day. It will take more planning and you will take fewer flights and more overnight buses. Banana pancakes and other street food will be a staple in your diet and dorms will put a roof over your head. But for travelers who are up to the challenge and enjoy bare bones travel then Thailand is a great spot to see just how cheap you can go.

Pack

As a modern and global country Thailand has most of the supplies, clothes and goods that you are used to finding at home. You can save on space and weight for your bags whether they are backpacks or rolling suitcases and plan to buy things for cheap there if you run out. For those who will be there for a while don't try to bring of your toiletries, plan to buy some toothpaste and shampoo when yours runs out. If you are worried about having enough socks then plan to do laundry halfway through your stay or buy another few pairs.

When traveling far from home it is tempting to bring all of your creature comforts along, the cute shoes that go with that shirt and a few extra pairs of socks in case you run out. However when you travel to any destination you run the risk of something being lost or stolen so leave your favorite clothes and belongings safe at home. Better to remember the full moon party as the best party of your life and not when you spent three hours searching the dark beach for your designer flip flops.

Since shopping is so popular in Thailand and there are so many different things to buy make sure to leave room in your bags and don't overload them so you have space to bring back souvenirs and gifts. It will also make traveling to the different regions easier if you are not carrying forty pounds of books, shoes and conditioner. It is also a good idea to leave some of your electronics at home to avoid weighing yourself down with camera lenses, chargers and extra batteries. Just one smart device and a camera with an empty memory card will be enough.

An important aspect to consider is the weather and what regions you will be visiting. If you are traveling to the north during the colder season from November to February, the temperatures will be at the lowest. For those hiking in the north and visiting mountain tops you will want to bring extra layers and thicker socks, it can drop to freezing at night. Conversely if you are on the islands during the hottest months, March to June, then you will want to pack lightweight clothing that is light in color and dries quickly. If your trip falls during the rainy season then pack some good rain gear that is breathes, it may be raining but it is still hot out. Consider picking up an umbrella once you arrive but pack a small rain poncho to tide you over until you find one. No matter the time of year it is a good idea to bring a hat and sunblock, good walking shoes and sunglasses.

The most important thing to pack is your spirit of adventure. Thailand is very different from the western world in a lot of wonderful ways and in some surprising ways too. As much time as you put into making the perfect itinerary things will not always go according to plan so be ready to go with the flow and know that it will be a great story for friends and family.

Go next

As part of the Southeast Asian countries that are frequented by backpackers and other overlanders, chances are good that you will visit Thailand in conjunction with a visit to Vietnam, Cambodia, Laos, Malaysia, and other neighboring countries. You can easily get to these countries by bus and by plane, both of which can be ultra low cost ways of travel and excellent adventures.

As you are planning your trip if you want to do some extra reading on Thailand to get an idea of what awaits there are many books that you can delve into for an insider's view. Check out *Mai Pen Rai Means Never Mind* by Carol Hollinger to read about her account of living in Thailand 30 years ago. Or to learn more about the Thai ways of life take a look at *Very Thai* by Philip Cornwel-Smith or *Culture Shock! Thailand* by Robert and Nanthapa Cooper. While you are still overseas you can Daniel Ziv and Guy Sharrett's *Bangkok Inside Out*, though it is now banned in Thailand due to some of the imagery. This book will give you the low-down on Thailand without the sugar coating.

Useful websites

Here are some handy websites for more information about visiting and getting around Thailand.

Background and history of Thailand

www.wikivoyage.org

www.wikipedia.org

www.tripadvisor.com

www.tourismthailand.org

www.travel.state.gov/content/passports/english/country/thailand.html

www.visahq.com

Hostels

www.hostelworld.com

www.hostelbookers.com

Hotels

www.agoda.com

www.booking.com

Homestays

www.airbnb.com

Place websites

www.visitchiangmai.com.au

www.bangkok.com

www.bangkok-city.com

www.kohlipe.net

www.kohlipethailand.com

www.phuket.net

www.gokohphiphi.com

www.kohphangan.com

www.fullmoonparty-thailand.com

www.kohsamui.com

www.kosamui.com

www.kohsamui.org

Transportation

www.bangkokmetro.co.th

http://www.thailandtrainticket.com

Flights

www.skyscanner.com

www.momondo.com

www.bravofly.com

Help

www.phuket-tourist-police-volunteers.com

To check out the rest of "*Thailand For Tourists*" go to Amazon and look for ir right now!

THAILAND
For Tourists

The Traveler's Guide to
Make the Most Out of Your Trip to Thailand
- Where to Go, Eat, Sleep & Party

DAGNY TAGGART & KATHERINE VOSS

Check Out My Other Books

Are you ready to exceed your limits? Then pick a book from the one below and start learning yet another new language.   I can't imagine anything more fun, fulfilling, and exciting!

If you'd like to see the entire list of language guides (there are a ton more!), go to:

>>**http://www.amazon.com/Dagny-Taggart/e/B00K54K6CS/**<<

About the Author

Dagny Taggart is a language enthusiast and polyglot who travels the world, inevitably picking up more and more languages along the way.

Taggart's true passion became learning languages after she realized the incredible connections with people that it fostered. Now she just can't get enough of it. Although it's taken time, she has acquired vast knowledge on the best and fastest ways to learn languages. But the truth is, she is driven simply by her motive to build exceptional links and bonds with others.

She is inspired everyday by the individuals she meets across the globe. For her, there's simply not anything as rewarding as practicing languages with others because she gets to make friends with people from all that come from a variety of cultures. This, in turn, has broadened her mind and thinking more than she would have ever imagined it could.

Of course, as a result of her constant travels, Taggart has become an expert on planning trips and making the most of time spent out of what she calls her "base" town. She jokes that she's practically at the nomad status now, but she's more content to live that way.

She knows how to live on a manageable budget weather she's in Paris or Phnom Penh. She knows how to seek out the adventures and thrills, no doubt, lying in wait at any city she visits. She knows that reflection on each every experience is significant if she wants to grow as a traveler and student of the world's cultures.

Because of this, Taggart chooses to share her understanding of languages and travel so that others, too, can experience the same life-altering benefits she has.

Printed in Great Britain
by Amazon.co.uk, Ltd.,
Marston Gate.